T0219764

Lecture Notes in Computer Science 9461

Commenced Publication in 1973
Founding and Former Series Editors:
Gerhard Goos, Juris Hartmanis, and Jan van Leeuwen

More information about this series at http://www.springer.com/series/7409

Ruichu Cai · Kang Chen
Liang Hong · Xiaoyan Yang
Rong Zhang · Lei Zou (Eds.)

Web Technologies and Applications

APWeb 2015 Workshops, BSD, WDMA, and BDAT
Guangzhou, China, September 18, 2015
Revised Selected Papers

 Springer

Editors
Ruichu Cai
Guangdong University of Technology
Guangzhou, Guangdong
China

Kang Chen
Research Institute of China Telecom Co.
Guangzhou
China

Liang Hong
Wuhan University
Wuhan
China

Xiaoyan Yang
Advanced Digital Sciences Center
Singapore
Singapore

Rong Zhang
East China Normal University
Shanghai
China

Lei Zou
Peking University
Beijing
China

ISSN 0302-9743   ISSN 1611-3349 (electronic)
Lecture Notes in Computer Science
ISBN 978-3-319-28120-9   ISBN 978-3-319-28121-6 (eBook)
DOI 10.1007/978-3-319-28121-6

Library of Congress Control Number: 2015950917

LNCS Sublibrary: SL3 – Information Systems and Applications, incl. Internet/Web, and HCI

Printed on acid-free paper

This Springer imprint is published by SpringerNature
The registered company is Springer International Publishing AG Switzerland

Workshop 1

International Workshop on Big Data Applications in Telecoms (BDAT 2015)

Introduction:

Big data has become ubiquitous in telecommunications. The great amount of telecom data challenges state-of-the-art data computation and analysis methods. The aim of this workshop is together experts in big data and to promote its applications in telecommunications.

Program Committee

Co-chairs

Ruichu Cai	Guangdong University of Technology, China
Kang Chen	China Telecom Co., China

Members

Hua Lu	Aalborg University, Denmark
Feng Li	Microsoft Research, USA
Ilaria Bartolini	University of Bologna, Italy
Joao Paulo Bartolo Gomes	I2R, Singapore
Baozhong Wang	China Telecom Co., China
Leong Hou U.	University of Macau, Macau
Raymond Wong	HKUST, Hong Kong, SAR China
Yong Xiang	China Telecom Co., China

Workshop 2

The First International Workshop on Big Social Data (BSD 2015)

Introduction:

The First International Workshop on Big Social Data (BSD 2015) targets research that focuses on all aspects of the greatest challenges and opportunities arising from big social data. Big social data refers to the data collected from human interactions through the Web and mobile devices. This dataset is a rich source of information; enabling new scientific, economic, and social studies.

The overall goals of the workshop are to bring people from different fields together, to foster the exchange of research ideas and results, and to encourage discussion on how to manage, analyze, and visualize big social data in different application domains and to understand the research challenges of this area. We believe that big social data is an emerging research topic that has not been served by a dedicated workshop in any of the main database conferences. It has many practical applications that still need further investigations and much research efforts from the database community. We believe that the BSD workshop will become a traditional annual meeting for the community of researchers in different topics of the field of big social data.

Honorary Chair

Cyrus Shahabi   University of Southern California, USA

Program Co-chairs

Liang Hong   Wuhan University, China
Lei Zou   Peking University, China

Program Committee Members

Luming Zhang   National University of Singapore, Singapore
Xiang Lian   University of Texas-Pan American, USA
Yu Zheng   Microsoft Research Asia, China
Wen Zhang   Wuhan University, China

Workshop 3

First International Workshop on Web Data Mining and Applications (WDMA 2015)

Introduction:

The Web is continuing to develop into the ultimate information repository of the world. Users publish and share textual documents as well as multimedia data on various websites including social network systems and Web portals. With tons of data created everyday on the Web, there is a growing interest in developing and applying data-mining techniques to discover useful knowledge from user-generated data on the Web. This workshop on Web Data Mining and Applications (WDMA 2015) aimed to contribute to the development of data-mining algorithms and applications for user-generated data on the Web.

Organizing Committee

Rong Zhang   East China Normal University, China
Xiaoyan Yang   Advanced Digital Sciences Center, Singapore

Program Committee

Zhihong Chong   Southeast University, China
Xiaofeng He   East China Normal University, China
Yue Kou   Northeastern University, China
Tiezheng Nie   Northeastern University, China
Xiang Shili   Institute for Infocomm Research, Singapore
Fang Yuan   Institute for Infocomm Research, Singapore
Minqi Zhou   East China Normal University, China

Organization

Steering Committee

Chair

Jeffrey Xu Yu   The Chinese University of Hong Kong, SAR China

Members

Masaru Kitsuregawa   University of Tokyo, Japanese
Jianzhong Li   Harbin Institute of Technology, China
Xuemin Lin   The University of New South Wales, Australia
Kyu-Young Whang   Korea Advanced Institute of Science and Technology, Korea
Ge Yu   Northeastern University, China
Yanchun Zhang   Victoria University, Australia
Aoying Zhou   East China Normal University, China
Xiaofang Zhou   The University of Queensland, Australia

Organizers

China Telecom

Guangdong University of Technology

Contents

WDMA

BDAT

A Method of Text Classification Combining Naive Bayes and the Similarity Computing Algorithms

Yinghan Hong[1(✉)], Guizhen Mai[2], Hui Zeng[1], and Cai Guo[1]

[1] Hanshan Normal University, Chaozhou 521041, Gugangdong, China
869810392@qq.com
[2] Guangdong University of Technology,
Guangzhou 510006, Gugangdong, China

Abstract. Text classification is one of the main issues in the big data analysis and research. In present, however, there is a lack of a universal algorithm model that can fulfill the requirement of both accuracy and efficiency of text classification. This paper proposes a method of text classification, which combines the Naive Bayes and the similarity computing algorithm. Firstly, the text information is cut into several word segmentation vectors by the Paoding Analyzer; then the Bayesian algorithm is employed to conduct the first-level directory classification to the text information; after that, the improved similarity computing algorithm is adopted to carry out the second-level directory classification. Finally, the algorithm model is tested with actual data, and the results are compared with those of Bayesian algorithm and similarity computing algorithm respectively. The results show that the proposed method achieves a higher precision rate.

Keywords: Naive Bayesian algorithm · Similarity computing algorithm · Precision

1 Introduction

Similarity computing, used to measure the degree of similarity between objects, is a basic calculation in data mining and natural language processing, whose key technology mainly includes two parts, that is, the characteristics of the objects and the similar relationship between features set [1, 2]. When it comes to information retrieval, recommendation system, or to judge whether the page is repeated, all of them are concerned with the similarity calculation between the objects or between objects and object collections. Nevertheless, due to different application scenarios, data size, time and space costs restrictions, selecting the method of similarity calculation can be various from condition to condition. Naïve Bayesian algorithm, one of the statistical classification methods, is a kind of algorithm using probability and statistics knowledge to classify. In many cases, Naïve Bayesian algorithm can be comparable with the Decision Tree classification algorithm and Neural Network algorithm, and this algorithm can be applied to large database, with simple method, high precision rate and high speed while in classification.

© Springer International Publishing Switzerland 2015
R. Cai et al. (Eds.): APWeb 2015 Workshops, LNCS 9461, pp. 3–14, 2015.
DOI: 10.1007/978-3-319-28121-6_1

Similarity computing algorithm and Naïve Bayesian algorithm have their own advantages and disadvantages, which mainly reflect on the precision and recall. The algorithm model requires higher precision rate and recall rate, but in fact there is no perfect algorithms can meet such requirements, with the cause of data complexity and lack of integrity [3–5]. In order to solve the above problems, we need to improve the existing algorithm model constantly, and try to find out appropriate scientific methods for data classification under the condition of specific data types [6, 7]. From a large amount of data obtained from previous experiments, we can conclude that in the classification of e-commerce goods, using Naïve Bayesian algorithm has higher precision and recall rate the first-level directory classification, while similarity computing algorithm the second-level directory classification. As is shown in the Tables 1, 2, we can combine them scientifically to make full use of the advantages of both algorithms, so that it can adapt to the data, and the precision rate of the entire data classification can be improved eventually.

Table 1. The Precision and Recall with NB and SC in the first-level directory classification

The first-level directory classification				
	Naive Bayesian algorithm		Similarity computing algorithm	
	Precision	Recall	Precision	Recall
pad	96.69 %	92.68 %	90.43 %	87.46 %
phone	90.16 %	92.14 %	84.05 %	81.86 %
air-conditioning	99.62 %	86.75 %	92.48 %	89.03 %
large-appliances-fitting	97.5 %	50.97 %	90.87 %	73.65 %
washer	97.80 %	71.70 %	89.19 %	84.22 %
women-shoes	86.76 %	89.73 %	75.34 %	72.91 %
kitchen	90.94 %	86.54 %	85.45 %	81.21 %
accessories	86.24 %	91.12 %	80.85 %	83.82 %
phone fitting	99.28 %	78.57 %	90.49 %	84.28 %
notebook	95.14 %	98.85 %	87.35 %	85.39 %
fridge	97.45 %	81.90 %	89.40 %	73.08 %
tv	98.41 %	89.56 %	92.94 %	80.43 %
women-clothing	77.90 %	86.28 %	70.48 %	72.92 %
vedio	95.0 %	84.16 %	87.18 %	80.74 %
man-clothing	89.84 %	73.85 %	80.33 %	78.92 %
children-clothing	95.71 %	80.0 %	87.58 %	75.29 %
digital-camera	87.97 %	97.77 %	80.44 %	75.72 %
man-shoes	89.90 %	85.81 %	82.93 %	78.85 %

Table 2. The Precision and Recall with NB and SC the second-level directory classification

The second-level directory classification(Taking an example of air-conditioning)				
	Naïve Bayesian algorithm		Similarity computing algorithm	
	Precision	Recall		Precision
Kelon	95.65 %	100 %	100 %	100 %
Whirlpo	100 %	100 %	100 %	100 %
Mitsubishi	100 %	97.06 %	100 %	100 %
YORK	100 %	100 %	100 %	100 %
Hisense	98.24 %	100 %	100 %	100 %
AUX	73.84 %	100 %	73.85 %	100 %
Hitachi	100 %	100 %	100 %	100 %
shinco	100 %	66.67 %	100 %	100 %
TCL	100 %	83.33 %	100 %	100 %
Midea	97.29 %	100 %	100 %	100 %
CHANGHONG	100 %	15.79 %	100 %	100 %
Galanz	100 %	17.65 %	100 %	100 %
Haier	81.44 %	100 %	100 %	100 %
CHIGO	87.80 %	90.0 %	100 %	100 %
DAIKIN	100 %	100 %	100 %	100 %
Gree	72.05 %	100 %	100 %	100 %
Chunlan	100 %	71.43 %	100 %	100 %

2 Preliminaries

2.1 Bayesian Classification Algorithm

A naïve Bayes classifier estimates the class-conditional probability by assuming that the attributes are conditionally independent, given the class label y. The conditional independence assumption can be formally stated as follows [8]:

$$p(X \backslash Y = y) = \prod_{i=1}^{d} p(Xi \backslash Y = y) \tag{1}$$

Where each attribute set X = {X1, X2, ..., Xd} consists of d attributes.

To classify a test record, the naïve Bayes classifier computes the posterior probality for each class Y:

$$p(Y \backslash X) = \frac{p(Y) \prod_{i=1}^{d} p(Xi \backslash Y)}{p(X)} \tag{2}$$

Since P(X) is fixed for every Y, it is sufficient to choose the class that maximizes the numerator term,

$$p(Y) \prod_{i=1}^{d} p(Xi\backslash Y) \tag{3}$$

2.2   Similarity Computing Algorithm

The cosine similarity, defined next, is one of the most common measure of document similarity. If x and y two document vectors, then

$$\cos(x,y) = \frac{x}{\|x\|} \cdot \frac{y}{\|y\|} = x'.y' \tag{4}$$

where x' = x/||x|| and y' = y/||y||. Dividing x and y by their lengths normalizes them to have a length of 1. This means that cosine similarity does not take the magnitude of the two data objects into account when computing similarity.

2.3   TF-IDF

TF-IDF is a common weighting technique used for information retrieval and text mining.

(1) Term frequency (TF) refers to the number of occurrences of a given term in the document. It is expressed as:

$$\mathrm{tf}_{i,j} = \frac{n_{i,j}}{\sum_k n_{k,j}} \tag{5}$$

Where ni, j represents the number of occurrences of the term in the document dj, and the denominator is the sum of the number of occurrences of all terms in the document dj.

(2) Inverse document frequency (IDF) is the indicator of the general importance of a term. The IDF of a particular term can be obtained through dividing the total number of documents by the number of documents that contain this term and then taking logarithm of the obtained quotient.

3   Algorithm Combining Naive Bayes and Similarity Computing

3.1   Algorithm Flowchart

By analyzing the advantages and disadvantages of the two algorithms of naive Bayes and similarity computing, the flow chart of the algorithm is shown in Fig. 1.

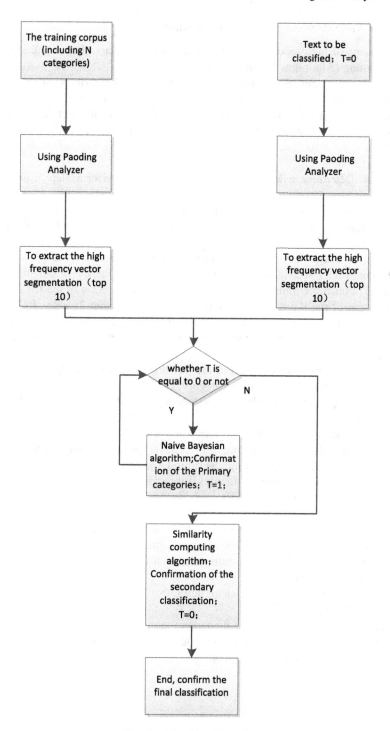

Fig. 1. Algorithm Flowchart

3.2   Step Analysis of Algorithm Implementation

(1) The steps of the proposed algorithm combining the Naive Bayes and similarity computing (Algorithm 1) are as follows:

Step 1: Input the list of the to-be-classified text information, store the text information as a data set in the database, and initialize $t = 0$;

Step 2: Use Paoding Analyzer for word segmentation of the text information;

Step 3: Extract feature words and select word segments with a higher frequency (the top 10 most frequent word segments) as the feature vector of the text information;

Step 4: Determine whether vector t equals 0. If so, perform Step 5; otherwise, perform Step 6;

Step 5: Use Bayesian categorization algorithm for matching (for details see Algorithm 2), and confirm the first-level directory classification of the text information; $t = 1$;

Step 6: Use text similarity algorithm for matching (for details see Algorithm 3), and confirm the second-level directory classification of the text information; $t = 0$;

Step 7: Finish the running and export the final classification of the text;

(2) The steps of the Bayes classification algorithm (Algorithm 2) are as follows [9]:

Step 1: Get ready to train the first-level directory, and prepare the test text;

Step 2: Start the training model, and loop through the text documents in the directory;

Step 3: Extract the feature term of the text document with Paoding Analyzer;

Step 4: Calculate $P(yi)$ for each category;

Step 5: Calculate the conditional probabilities of all divisions for each feature property;

Step 6: Calculate $P(x\backslash yi)P(yi)$ for each category;

Step 7: Take the term of maximum $P(x\backslash yi)P(yi)$ as the category of X;

(3) The steps of the text computing algorithm (Algorithm 3) are as follows [10]:

Step 1: Get ready to train the first-level directory, and prepare the test text;

Step 2: Start the training model, and loop through the text documents in the directory;

Step 3: Extract the feature term of the text document with Paoding Analyzer;

Step 4: Count the number of each feature term;

Step 5: Count the TF of the feature term, that is, the number of a single feature term/total TF in the text;

Step 6: Count the IDF of the feature term, that is, the number of a single feature term/total TF in the directory;

Step 7: Calculate the vector of the feature term, TF*IDF;

Step 8: Train the feature vectors of the text mode, and calculate the cosine of the angle between vectors (text similarity);

4   Experiment and Analysis

4.1   Description of Experimental Data Set

In this paper, the experimental dataset was the product information obtained from Jingdong, Tmall, Taobao and other e-commerce sites. By use of Web crawler software, we collected the information of common products, including 19 first-level categories such as phone and notebook, and 555 s-level categories such as phone- > coolpad and notebook- > thinkpad, as well as 7784 pieces of product information in total such as phone- > coolpad- > Lenovo E135 (3359A61) and notebook- > thinkpad- > Coolpad 7268 (white).

4.2   Training Data Model

(1) Use Paoding Analyzer to cut the product information into word segments

For example, Information of common products :Mobile phones > mobile communication > > cool > 5930 【5930】 cool cool cool 5930 telecom 3 g mobile phones (white) CDMA2000 /GSM dual mode dual stay 【market price evaluation】.

The vector set obtained by Paoding Analyzer was as follows:

【Mobile phones mobile communications cool cool cool cool 5930 5930 5930 telecom 3 g 3 g mobile phone white cdma 2000 cdma2000 GSM dual mode dual market price evaluation 】.

(2) Extract feature terms with a high frequency (top 10) is shown in the Table 3.

Table 3. Product Code (p000001)

Word Segmentation	times	Whether to choose
Mobile phones	4	Y
Coolpad	4	Y
5930	3	Y
mobile communications	1	Y
telecom	1	Y
3	1	Y
3 g	1	Y
g	1	Y
white	1	Y
cdma	1	Y
2000	1	N
cdma 2000	1	N
gsm	1	N
dual mode	1	N
dual stay	1	N
market	1	N
price	1	N
evaluation	1	N

(3) Use Bayesian algorithm to conduct first-level classification for product p000001. Classification result: phone (01);

(4) Use similarity computing algorithm to conduct second-level classification for product p000001. Classification result: Coolpad (03);

(5) Finally classify product p000001 into phone–> coolpad (0103), and end this program;

(6) Orderly classify the 7784 products in the data set, and eventually establish the training data model library.

4.3   Data Testing Process

(1) 284 pieces of product text information were extracted from the test set, and loop test of the product information was performed with the algorithm combining Naive Bayes and similarity computing. The program was run for 1666 ms, determining 281 correct results (correct rate of 98.94 %) and 3 incorrect ones (incorrect rate of 1.06 %). As shown in Table 4:

Table 4.   The Result of Algorithm combining Naive Bayes and similarity computing

		Classified as A...L											
		A	B	C	D	E	F	G	H	I	J	K	L	M
	A	8	0	0	0	0	0	0	0	0	0	0	0	0
	B	0	3	0	0	0	0	0	0	0	0	0	0	0
	C	0	0	13	0	0	0	0	0	0	0	0	0	0
	D	0	0	0	8	0	0	0	0	0	0	0	0	0
	E	0	0	0	0	5	0	0	0	0	0	0	0	0
	F	1	0	0	0	0	94	0	0	1	0	0	0	0
Item	G	0	0	0	0	0	0	90	0	1	0	0	0	0
	H	0	0	0	0	0	0	0	21	0	0	0	0	0
	I	0	0	0	0	0	0	0	0	1	0	0	0	0
	J	0	0	0	0	0	0	0	0	0	10	0	0	0
	K	0	0	0	0	0	0	0	0	0	0	18	0	0
	L	0	0	0	0	0	0	0	0	0	0	0	10	0
	M	0	0	0	0	0	0	0	0	0	0	0	0	0
	Item-total	9	3	13	8	5	94	90	21	3	10	18	10	0
	total	284												
Result	correct	281												
	Incorrect	3												
	Running	1666(ms)												

Table 5. The Result of Naive Bayes Algorithm

		Classified as A...L											
		A	B	C	D	E	F	G	H	I	J	K	L	M
Item	A	8	0	0	0	0	0	0	0	0	1	0	0	0
	B	0	3	0	0	0	0	0	0	0	0	0	0	0
	C	0	0	13	0	0	1	0	0	0	0	0	0	0
	D	0	0	0	8	0	1	5	0	0	0	0	0	0
	E	0	0	0	0	5	0	0	0	0	0	0	0	0
	F	1	0	0	0	0	90	0	0	1	0	0	0	0
	G	0	0	0	0	0	0	80	0	1	1	0	0	0
	H	0	0	0	0	0	0	0	21	0	0	0	0	0
	I	0	0	0	0	0	1	0	0	1	0	0	0	0
	J	0	0	0	0	0	0	5	0	0	8	0	0	0
	K	0	0	0	0	0	0	0	0	0	0	18	0	0
	L	0	0	0	0	0	1	0	0	0	0	0	10	0
	M	0	0	0	0	0	0	0	0	0	0	0	0	0
	Item-total	9	3	13	8	5	94	90	21	3	10	18	10	0
Result	total	284												
	correct	265												
	Incorrect	19												
	Running time	1876(ms)												
	Precision	93.31%												

(2) Information of 284 products was extracted from the test set, and loop test of the product information was performed with the Naive Bayes algorithm.The program was run for 1876 ms, determining 265 correct results (correct rate of 93.31 %) and 19 incorrect ones (incorrect rate of 6.69 %). As shown in Table 5:

(3) Information of 284 products was extracted from the test set, and loop test of the product information was performed with the similarity computing algorithm.The program was run for 1977 ms, determining 260 correct results (correct rate of 91.55 %) and 24 incorrect ones (incorrect rate of 8.45 %). As shown in Table 6:

4.4 Analysis of Test Results

The algorithm combining Naive Bayes and similarity computing, the Bayesian algorithm, and the similarity computing algorithm were respectively used to test the data set. Results are shown in Figs. 2 and 3:

Table 6. The Result of similarity computing Algorithm

		Classified as A...L											
		A	B	C	D	E	F	G	H	I	J	K	L	M
Item	A	8	0	0	0	0	0	0	0	0	0	0	0	0
	B	0	3	0	0	0	0	5	0	0	0	0	0	0
	C	0	0	13	0	0	5	0	0	0	0	0	0	0
	D	0	0	0	8	0	2	0	0	0	0	0	0	0
	E	0	0	0	0	5	0	0	0	0	0	0	0	0
	F	0	0	0	0	0	80	0	0	1	0	0	0	0
	G	0	0	0	0	0	0	82	0	1	0	0	0	0
	H	0	0	0	0	0	0	0	21	0	0	0	0	0
	I	0	0	0	0	0	4	0	0	1	0	0	0	0
	J	0	0	0	0	0	0	3	0	0	10	0	0	0
	K	0	0	0	0	0	0	0	0	0	0	18	0	0
	L	0	0	0	0	0	3	0	0	0	0	0	10	0
	M	0	0	0	0	0	0	0	0	0	0	0	0	0
	Item-total	9	3	13	8	5	94	90	21	3	10	18	10	0
Result	total	284												
	correct	260												
	Incorrect	24												
	Running time	1977(ms)												
	Precision	91.55%												

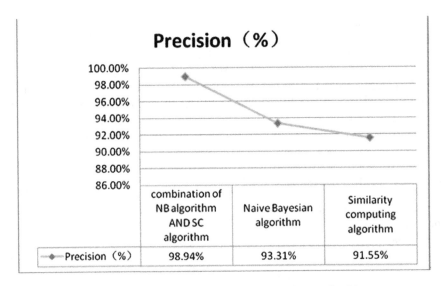

Fig. 2. Comparison results of the Precision of three algorithms

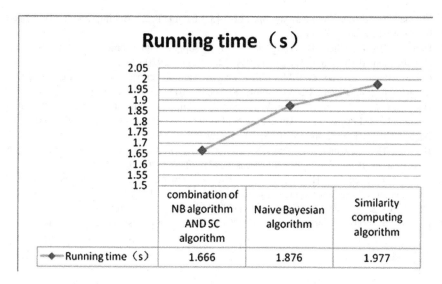

Fig. 3. Comparison results of the running time of three algorithms

By comparing the three algorithms in accuracy and running time, the results showed that the algorithm combining Naive Bayes and similarity computing had a good performance in accuracy and running time.

5   Conclusion

Although text categorization is a research hotspot, there is currently no scientific algorithm to adapt to the categorization of all texts, as each algorithm has its own advantages and disadvantages. In this paper, first-level and second-level classifications were conducted for common digital products, and an algorithm that combines the Naive Bayes and similarity computing was proposed to solve the accuracy problems in text information classification, with relatively obvious effect. Due to the limitations of the test data size and scenarios, in further studies, massive dataset will be used for testing and a more appropriate algorithm will be developed to solve the problems, so as to achieve the desired results.

Acknowledgements. This work was supported by Science and Technology Planning Project of Guangdong Province, China (2015A030401101), (2012B040500034).

References

1. Steinbach, M., Kumar, V.: Introduction To Data Mining. Pand-Ning Tan Press (2010)
2. Ju, C., Yin, X., Xu, C.: Bayesian classification algorithm of dynamic data stream based on bootstrap. Comput. Eng. Appl. **47**(8), 118–121 (2011)

3. Mitchell, T.M.: Machine Learning, pp. 112–143. Machine Press, Beijing (2003). (Translated by Zeng, H., Zhang, Y., et al.)

4. Hao, Z., He, L., Chen, B., Yang, X.: A linear support higher-order tensor machine for classification. IEEE Trans. Image Process. **22**(7), 2911–2920 (2013)

5. Cai, R., Zhang, Z., Hao, Z.: BASSUM: a Bayesian semi-supervised method for classification feature selection. Pattern Recogn. **44**(4), 811–820 (2011)

6. Hao, Z., Cheng, J., Cai, R., Wen, W., Wang, L.: Chinese sentiment classification based on the sentiment drop point. In: Huang, D.-S., Gupta, P., Wang, L., Gromiha, M. (eds.) ICIC 2013. CCIS, vol. 375, pp. 55–60. Springer, Heidelberg (2013)

7. Hao, Z., He, L., Chen, B., Yang, X.: A linear support higher-order tensor machine for classification. IEEE Trans. Image Process. **22**(7), 2911–2920 (2013)

8. Yufeng, D., Zhenzhen, H., Fei, J., et al.: Study on semantic markup of species description text in chinese based on auto-learning rules. New Technol. Libr. Inf. Serv. **5**, 41–47 (2012)

9. http://www.360doc.com/content/13/0809/13/891660_305827106.shtml

10. http://www.cnblogs.com/leoo2sk/archive/2010/09/17/naive-bayesian-classifier.html

An Empirical Study of a Large Scale Online Recommendation System

Huazheng Fu[1]($^{\boxtimes}$), Kang Chen[1], and Jianbing Ding[2]

[1] Guangzhou Research Institute, China Telecom Corporation Ltd., Beijing, China
{fuhuaz,chenkang}@gsta.com
[2] Advanced Digital Sciences Center,
Illinois at Singapore Pte. Ltd., Singapore, Singapore
jianbing.d@adsc.com.sg

Abstract. The online recommendation service has a wide range of usages for the various applications of Telecommunication companies. For such applications, the user base is usually tremendous with a variety of user characteristics and habits. Therefore, it is a challenge to achieve the high click through rate (CTR) for the online recommendations. In this paper, we proposed an approach of combining the technologies of ensemble trees and logistic regression (LR). The ensemble trees are effective in capturing the joint information of different features, which are then used by the LR scheme. In addition, to deal with the scalability issues, we implemented our system with both Apache Storm (for real-time prediction and classification) and Apache Spark (for fast off-line model training). A group of experiments were carried out with real-world data sets and the results show the efficiency and effectiveness of our proposed approach.

1 Introduction

With the rapid development of mobile Internet, intelligent terminal, cloud computing and Internet of things, Telecommunication industry has experienced a substantial increase in traffic volume and data intensity. Take China Telecom as an example, it has a bunch of systems, e.g. Customer Relationship Management (CRM), Business Intelligence (BI), Business and Operation Support System (BOSS), etc., which have recorded more than 0.75 billion pieces of user interaction information, and this number keeps increasing every day. In fact, these meta data contains very rich and valuable information related to the customers, such as the customer profile, call detail records (CDRs), web-surfing traffics, usage of data services, usages of intelligent terminals and so on. In this sense, China Telecom is surely facing the big data challenges, as known as "4V": *volume, variety, value and velocity.*

In Telecommunication industry, the primary use of these meta data is for delicacy traffic management. The commercial values of the big data applications are reflected in two aspects: (a) have a deeper understanding of customer behaviors; and (b) help on calibrated-marketing [1].

© Springer International Publishing Switzerland 2015
R. Cai et al. (Eds.): APWeb 2015 Workshops, LNCS 9461, pp. 15–25, 2015.
DOI: 10.1007/978-3-319-28121-6_2

For (a), since there is a large amount of customers' terminal information, their web surfing records of mobile devices, and other related meta data, the traditional approach is to establish the calibrated classification model for customers. With the help of deep packet inspection (DPI) technology, it is able to labeling the different groups of customers based on their online behaviors, which helps the service providers to obtain the complete customers' "portraits" and get a thorough understanding of customers' personal preferences and needs. The outcome of (a) is then utilized for advertizement and establishing the precise matching between the customers and the service packages, terminal device types and so on; and also for satisfying the customized user demands.

However, it is still a challenge how to properly use these data for delicacy traffic management. For example, when a customer logins the online business office of a Telecom company, how can we make prediction on his/her behaviors, i.e., whether or not to click on those links which are produced by the online recommendation algorithm?

This is actually a classification problem which needs real-time processing. The target is to find out what users are most likely interested in a very short time period. There are a good number of state-of-art approaches with acceptable performance proposed. Out of these, the approach which combines the ensemble trees and the probabilistic sparse linear classifier is the most suitable one for achieving our purpose.

However, all these approaches involves the model training phase, which is too time-consuming to meet the low latency requirement for the online recommendation systems. Therefore, in our design and implementation, we make the system into two separate modules, the offline data training, and the online recommendation, which can definitely run in parallel. We observe that the new features generated by the combined model earns higher AUC measure.

As the data volume is huge, in order to process as quick as possible, we choose to use Apache Spark, a Lightning-fast cluster computing engine for dealing with the offline data training module. However, due to the rigorous constraints on the response time of the online recommendation module, we choose to use Apache Storm for this module. Some other popular systems like Hadoop and Spark streaming are not taken into consideration because of their long processing delay for the inputs.

The paper is organized as follows. In Sect. 2, we begin with discussing the related work about CTR prediction. In Sect. 3, we describe the proposed algorithms. We introduce the implementation details in Sect. 4, and the experimental settings and results in Sect. 5. Section 6 concludes the work.

2   Related Work

In the machine learning research community, the CTR (click through rate) prediction problem is becoming more and more important. Recently, many people have proposed different models and methodologies for CTR prediction. For example, Neter et al. [2] proposed to use logistic regression, Richardson et al. [3]

and Graepel *et al.* [4] proposed to train the standard classifiers based on concatenation of the user and the ad features. Some other researchers suggested
models which use prior knowledge like the inherent hierarchical information in
log-loss models [5] or LR models [6]. In [7], Menon *et al.* used a matrix factorization approach without utilizing the user features. In [8], Yan *et al.* proposed
a coupled group lasso (CGL) model to integrate the conjunction information
from the user as well as the ad features. In [9], Stern *et al.* raised a probabilistic
model which used user and item features together with collaborative filter information. It mapped user and item features into lower dimensions and use inner
product to measure the similarity. In [10], the authors proposed a method which
use boosted decision trees to transform all the features to binary values which
were used for LR training. However, only use the transformed features may lose
important information for the classifier. Because LR model is easy to implement,
it is now becoming one of the most popular models for CTR prediction problem.
However, LR is a linear model, where the contribution made by the input features to the final prediction results are independent. In consequence, it cannot
capture the underlying connections among features. Better performance can be
achieved by applying the ensemble trees to capture the underlying connections
among features, which is then used for the LR training.

3   Algorithm Description

This section proposes a combined model structure: the concatenation of ensemble
trees and a probabilistic sparse linear classifier. In the following, we will introduce
how we combine the two schemes properly.

When transforming the input features to improve the accuracy of a linear
classifier, there are two possible ways [10]: (a) group the continuous features into

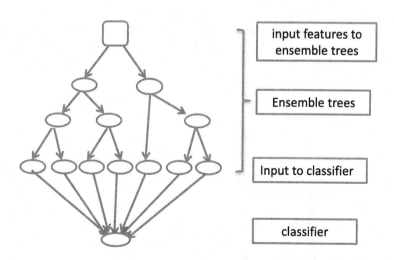

Fig. 1. The overview of the hybrid approach.

discrete bins, and (b) build tuple features. In the former case, the bin index was treated as a categorical feature from which the linear classifier can learn a piece-wise constant non-linear map. In the latter case, the Cartesian product of the categorical features and the joint binning of the continuous features is calculated to build the tuple features which are later useful for the linear classifier.

As is known that the ensemble trees scheme can realize both (a) and (b) discussed above, therefore it is a powerful and convenient tool to transform features of the linear classifiers.x In an ensemble tree, each individual subtree is treated as a categorical feature which is the index of the leaf node where an instance ends up. For example, consider the ensemble trees in Fig. 1. It has 2 subtrees. The left subtree has 4 leaf nodes while the right one has 3 leaf nodes. If an instance ends up at the third leaf node of the left subtree and the first leaf node of the right subtree, the result new feature produced by the ensemble trees will be a binary vector with values [0,0,1,0,1,0,0]. Each element of this binary vector is actually an indicator of the occurrence of the input instance to the corresponding leaf node. The ensemble trees can be realized as the gradient boosted decision trees (GBDT) [11], the random forest trees, and etc. In each learning iteration of the ensemble trees, a new tree is created and a binary vector is produced by it. We can take the ensemble trees based transformation as a supervised feature encoding whose functionality is to select those features that are more important to the classifier and jointly convert them into a compact binary-valued vector. A traversal from the root node to a leaf node represents a combination of some features. The weights of the rule set can be learnt by conducting a linear regressing on these binary vectors [10]. In addition, the ensemble trees are usually trained in a batch manner.

4   System Implementation

In this section, we introduce how we implement the online classification application with the Storm stream processing engine (SPE). At first, we give a brief introduction of the Apache Storm [12] SPE. Secondly, we present the key points of implementing the online classification module on Storm. At last, we describe how the online module interacts with the offline learning module, which will be implemented with the Apache Spark [13].

4.1   The Apache Storm SPE

Storm is a distributed real-time computation system open source by twitter. In Storm, each real-time application is represented by a directed graph (called topology in Storm), of which the vertices are user-defined operators which encapsulate computation logics and the edges define the data-transmitting path, pointing from the upstream operator to the downstream operator. Note that one characteristic of Storm is that such a directed graph can be a general one, hence this are no topological constraints, e.g., it allows loops (cyclic) and each operator can have multiple upstream operators and/or multiple downstream operators, too.

There are two types of operators pre-defined by Storm. One type with special API design, called spout, is acting as the role of the data source, which mainly concerns of retrieving data from dedicated storage (file or memory) and feeding them into the application topology. The other type, called bolt, is designed to serve more general purpose. It actually can be viewed as an abstraction of any kind of computation logic implementation.

4.2   Online Classification Application on Storm

There are two major functionalities of the online classification application: (a) quick response: compute and return the classification results requested by the user in real time; and (b) online model training: take the feedback data as the input to training the model and the coefficients, and live update the corresponding classifier.

Figure 2 illustrates the topology of the proposed online classification application. It consists of two spouts (Query spout and Feedback spout) and three bolts (Feature Extractor, Trainer and Classifier). To make a reliable and scalable system, we adopt the Kafka [14] as the implementation of the message queues, i.e., Storm spouts continuously read data from the Kafka queue, and feed them into the subsequent bolts to process. Since there are two different types of input data, we have created two pairs of spout and the corresponding Kafka queue for each of them, e.g. Query spout for the user classification requests and Feedback spout for the feedback data. The spouts encapsulate every input data message to be a Tuple, which will then be sent to the Feature Extractor Bolt.

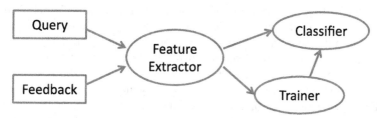

Fig. 2. Illustration of the topology of the proposed online classification application.

Feature extractor bolt: On receiving the input tuple from either the Query spout or the Feedback spout, the Feature Extractor applies the ensemble trees approach on extracting features. According to the description of the transformation algorithm in Sect. 3, for each input tuple, every decision tree generates a one dimensional sparse vector. Consequently, we can compress the output data of this bolt in an efficient way: to record the index of each non-zero element of the decision trees only, which helps to largely decrease the total data size to transmit through the network. In addition, each input tuple carries its sender information, say, the Query spout (respectively the Feedback spout), which is used by the Feature Extractor Bolt for choosing the correct downstream bolt, say the Classifier bolt (the Trainer bolt) to send the processed tuples.

Trainer bolt: Take the feedback data as the input, and based on the current coefficients of the LR model in the Classifier bolt, the Trainer bolt trains and updates the LR model. The training algorithm is very time consuming, thus to increase the throughput of the training phase, we apply the batch processing method. In particular, we allocate a separate memory space for buffering the input feedback tuples. Only when the total number of buffered tuples reaches a pre-defined threshold, will a dedicated thread be started to run the training algorithm. Finally, the Trainer sends these training results to the Classifier bolt after data serialization.

Classifier bolt: It takes input tuples from two upstream bolts. When the inputs are those user classification requests sent from the Feature extractor, it executes the classification job by using the LR model, and sends the results back to the user; when the inputs are from the Trainer bolt, it simply replaces the coefficients of the LR model with the input ones.

4.3 Interact with Spark

The supervised classification mostly consists of two phases, the training phase and the classifying phase. The former is delay insensitive, but shall be scalable and robust when the input data size is tremendous. The latter however, is delay sensitive, which means the response time for answering the user requests shall be as little as possible.

In our case, we have implemented the construction algorithm of the ensemble trees with Apache Spark. In the meantime, we utilize these ensemble trees to carry out fast feature extractions in the Feature extractor bolt. A technical challenge shows up when we try to achieve both: (a) keep the application topology running and unaffected; and (b) keep the ensemble trees up-to-date in real time.

HDFS (Hadoop distributed filesystem) [15] is therefore used to tackle this problem (as shown in Fig. 3). At first, we use Spark to run the ensemble trees construction algorithm, and serialize the newly generated ensemble trees onto the HDFS. During the initialization of Feature extractor bolt, the Storm metric API is called to register a temporal task, whose duty is to check the updates on the HDFS periodically. If there are updates, a separate thread will be started by the bolt to load the new generated ensemble trees from the HDFS in an asynchronous mode.

Fig. 3. Illustration of coordination among Storm, Spark and HDFS.

5   Experiment and Results

We implemented all proposed solution based on Apache Strom [12] v0.9.3 and Apache Spark [13] v1.2.0. The experiments were run on a cluster of 7 IBM servers, 4 of which were equipped with an Intel Xeon quad-core 2.53 GHz CPU and 32 GB of RAM, while others were equipped with an Intel Xeon dual-core 1.80 GHz CPU and 18 GB of RAM. We allocate one server to run as the master node, which hosts the Storm Nimbus. We choose 4 power servers to run spark, one as the master, the other three as slaves which have 8 GB of RAM and 16 cores. The Apache Kafka [14] is allocated on 3 servers and zookeeper 4 servers.

The dataset we use is CTR prediction from Kaggle Display Advertising Challenge. The first column is the label (click or not clock) for each instance. There are 24,004,662 instances in the dataset which has 13 numerical features and 26 categorical features. In our experiment, we choose 70 percent of the dataset for training the hybrid model and the remaining 30 percent for testing purpose. We apply the hot encoding approach in the pre-processing phase to encode the categorical features, and set the minimum distinct value to be 4 million, i.e. only features with more than 4 million distinct values will be encoded and kept.

In the following, we show the experiments in which the hybrid model demonstrated above is used. We first run experiments to evaluate the accuracy of different classification schemes on the dataset. We then investigate on the training time of these schemes. At last, we running experiment on Storm to show the relationship between the query arrival rate and the average response time.

The classification accuracy We carry out experiments to demonstrate the effect of including tree features as part of the input to the linear model. In this experiment, we compare the five schemes:

(a) LR model with original features (LR only);
(b) Random forest with original features (random forest only);
(c) GBDT with original features (GBDT only);
(d) LR model with features produced by GBDT (GBDT with LR);
(e) LR model with features produced by random forest (random forest with LR).

The Area-Under-ROC (AUC) is used to test the performance of the models. AUC is a good metric when we are to measure the ranking quality without considering calibration. A larger AUC value means a more accurate model, hence the better classification results. AUC value of three different models on the testing dataset is listed in Table 1.

The total processing time for model training In this set of experiments, we investigate the total processing time for model training spent by different schemes. The flow of the training process is: at first, we use the numerical features and transformed categorical features to train the ensemble trees. Secondly, the ensemble trees are used to produce the binary vectors. Lastly, the binary vectors together with the numerical features and the encoded categorical features are used to train the LR model where the Limited-memory BFGS algorithm [16] was used.

Table 1. Classification accuracy comparison on five schemes.

Scheme	AUC (relative value)
Random forest only	94.5 %
Random forest with LR	98.9 %
LR only	96.2 %
GBDT only	95.3 %
GBDT with LR	100.0 %

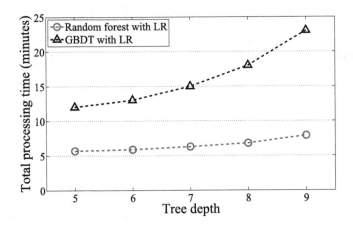

Fig. 4. The total processing time changing with different tree depth.

The settings of Spark applications were as follows: the total number of executors are set to 40, driver memory is 2 GB, and executor memory is 8 GB. The total processing time here includes both the pre-processing time and the model training time. We study the sensitivity of the tree depth and the number of different trees to the total processing time of the two schemes, random forest with LR versus GBDT with LR. The results are plotted in Figs. 4 and 5.

According to the results in Table 1, Figs. 4 and 5, we observe that GBDT with LR earns the highest accuracy, however, it spends much longer training time than the random forest with LR scheme. The results indicate that the choice of GBDT with LR or the random forest with LR depends on the application context: when it is insensitive to the training time while sensible with accuracy, GBDT with LR is the better choice; Oppositely, random forest with LR will be more preferred.

Next, we test the performance of the online classification application run on the Storm with different arrival rate of the online requests raised by users. Figure 6 shows the curve of the corresponding average response time.

We observe from Fig. 6 that (a) the processing speed is really fast on Storm and the response time is less than 5 ms when the request arrival rate reaches 50 K per second; and (b) the average response time increases super-linear to the

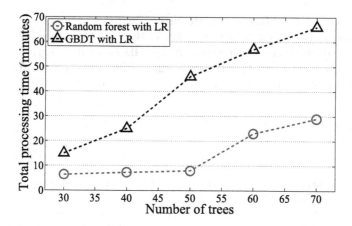

Fig. 5. The total processing time changing with the number of trees.

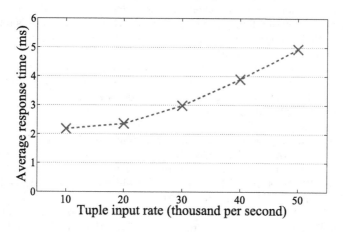

Fig. 6. The average response time changing with the tuple arrival rate.

arrival rate. This suggests that to keep the average response time under a certain threshold, far more resources shall be allocated at a higher request rate.

6   Conclusion

In this paper, we have studied and proposed a hybrid way (batching working with streaming processing) to implementing the online recommendation system with Apache Spark (for fast offline model training), Apache Storm (for quick answering users' online classification requests), and Hadoop file system (for data sharing and updating). This architecture helps enhancing the overall performance, in terms of the response time to the users' requests, the processing time for model training and updating, and the efficiency of the resource utilization.

Based on our hybrid framework, we also evaluated a group of online classification schemes. The experiment results imply that the choice on these different schemes shall depend on the using context, e.g. GBDT with LR earns the highest accuracy at the cost of long training time while random forest with LR earns the second highest in accuracy but spends less training time than GBDT with LR.

References

1. Huang, X.: Four directions of big data analytics in telecommunication industry. J. Telecommun. Tech. **6** (2013)
2. Neter, J., Kutner, M.H., Nachtsheim, C.J. Wasserman, W.: Applied linear statistical models. Irwin Chicago, vol. 4 (1996)
3. Richardson, M., Dominowska, E., Ragno, R.: Predicting clicks: estimating the click-through rate for new ads. In: Proceedings of the 16th international conference on World Wide Web, pp. 521–530. ACM (2007)
4. Graepel, T., Candela, J.Q., Borchert, T., Herbrich, R.: Web-scale bayesian click-through rate prediction for sponsored search advertising in microsoft's bing search engine. In: Proceedings of the 27th International Conference on Machine Learning (ICML- 2010), pp. 13–20 (2010)
5. Agarwal, D., Agrawal, R., Khanna, R., Kota, N.: Estimating rates of rare events with multiple hierarchies through scalable log-linear models. In: Proceedings of the 16th ACM SIGKDD international conference on Knowledge discovery and data mining, pp. 213–222. ACM (2010)
6. Lee, K.C., Orten, B.B., Dasdan, A., Li, W.: Estimating conversion rate in display advertising from past performance data, uS Patent App. 13/584,545, August 2012
7. Menon, A.K., Chitrapura, K.P., Garg, S., Agarwal, D., Kota, N.: Response prediction using collaborative filtering with hierarchies and side-information. In: Proceedings of the 17th ACM SIGKDD International Conference on Knowledge Discovery and Data Mining, pp. 141–149. ACM (2011)
8. Yan, L., Li, W.J., Xue, G.R., Han, D.: Coupled group lasso for web-scale ctr prediction in display advertising. In: Proceedings of the 31st International Conference on Machine Learning (ICML-2014), pp. 802–810 (2014)
9. Stern, D.H., Herbrich, R., Graepel, T.: Matchbox: large scale online bayesian recommendations. In: Proceedings of the 18th International Conference on World Wide Web, p. 111120. ACM(2009)
10. He, X., Pan, J., Jin, O., Xu, T., Liu, B., Xu, T., Shi, Y., Atallah, A., Herbrich, R., Bowers S, et al., Practical lessons from predicting clicks on ads at facebook. In: Proceedings of 20th ACM SIGKDD Conference on Knowledge Discovery and Data Mining, pp. 1–9. ACM (2014)
11. Gradient-Boosted Decision Trees, https://spark.apache.org/docs/1.2.1/mllib-ensembles.html#gradient-boosted-trees-gbts
12. Toshniwal, A., Taneja, S., Shukla, A., Ramasamy, K., Patel, J.M., Kulkarni, S., Jackson, J., Gade, K., Fu, M., Donham J. et al., Storm@ Twitter. In: Proceedings of ACM SIGMOD, pp. 147–156 (2014)
13. Zaharia, M., Chowdhury, M., Das, T., Dave, A., Ma, J., McCauley, M., Franklin, M.J., Shenker, S., Stoica, I.: Resilient distributed datasets: a fault-tolerant abstraction for in-memory cluster computing. In: Proceedings of the 9th USENIX conference on Networked Systems Design and Implementation. USENIX Association, pp. 2–2 (2012)

14. Kreps, J., Narkhede, N., Rao, J. et al.: Kafka: a distributed messaging system for log processing. In: Proceedings of 6th International Workshop on Networking Meets Databases (NetDB), Athens, Greece (2011)
15. HDFS, http://hadoop.apache.org/docs/r1.2.1/hdfs_design.html
16. Limited-memory BFGS, http://en.wikipedia.org/wiki/Limited-memory_BFGS

Application of Big Data Processing Technology in the Intelligent Network Management System

Pingli Zhou[✉], Zhiming Yang, Ling Li, and Shipeng Qiu

China Telecom Corporation Ltd. Guangzhou Research Institute,
Guangzhou, China
{zhoupl,yangzm,lil,qiusp}@gsta.com

Abstract. In this paper, according to the requirements of China Telecom's Network Planning and intelligent platform construction technology, we describe how to use big data technology to improve the processing efficiency of the massive network operation data, then analyze the characteristics and processing requirements of various data in the Intelligent Network Management system, propose reasonable solutions for large data processing, provide a guide for data processing of Network Operation Data Center in Intelligent Network Management platform in China Telecom.

Keywords: Intelligent network management · Big data · Data analysis

1 Introduction

In order to solve the problems of the network management system in the business and service support, centralized data operation, efficiency, China Telecom in 2012 began the future network management system (i.e., Intelligent Network Management System, abbr. INMS) research, in 2013 developed a series of standards and technical specifications and launched a pilot construction, in 2014, deployed it in the entire network. Constructing INMS, not only supports network intensive maintenance, operation and maintenance to operational transformation and a series of corporate strategic requirements, but also focuses on operating data centralization of the whole network to carry out big data applications based on the data. Therefore, the INMS will become intelligent data-centric network management system, to achieve data centralized cloud-based storage resource pools, sharing applications, data operations, massive data collection, storage, computing technology approach becomes especially important distinctions.

The INMS in the acquisition of the massive operation data for processing technology were discussed, hoping to certain guiding role for the INM platform Data Center construction in China Telecom.

2 The Concept of INMS

INMS is China Telecom's network management architecture with network management service platform and plug-in applications based on IT cloud infrastructure. Its objectives are to achieve a unified monitoring, one-stop operation, comprehensive

R. Cai et al. (Eds.): APWeb 2015 Workshops, LNCS 9461, pp. 26–34, 2015.
DOI: 10.1007/978-3-319-28121-6_3

analysis and end-to-end service through five core capabilities, i.e. intelligent sensing, intelligent control, intelligent management, intelligent analysis and intelligent business operations support.

INMS realizes horizontal-integration and vertical-flat architecture by breaking through the limitation of traditional Network management chimney. It maximizes network management value through centralized data, unified operation and management, network management capacity sharing. In order to reuse the capacity of legacy systems, it was well designed in style of SOA and with "plug-in" technology to integrate those systems. The INMS is comprised of 15 nodes, including the headquarter node and 14 province nodes, which are constructed in accordance with the unified technical architecture and standards, and interconnected through the distributed service bus, to achieve data centralization housing and sharing, and to deliver the services to where they are needed.

The INMS architecture is shown in Fig. 1. It includes panoramic view, service pool, data center, service bus, adaptation platform. The network data center is responsible for storing, transforming and accessing the network resource data and the network operation data which covers all kinds of data produced by network itself and network operators, including alarm, configuration, performance, data flow, log, calling bill, signal log, test data. Because the everyday-increment of those data is hundreds-TByte-level, therefore how to process those massive data and mining its value are currently the most valuable and most challenging requirements.

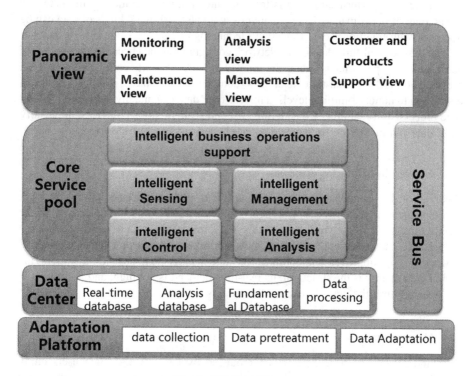

Fig. 1. INMS architecture

3 Data Classification and Processing Requirements

According to mode of data storage, data processing and use the different methods of data, the network operation data mainly divided into real-time data, converging data for analysis and usage data in the data center.

3.1 Real-Time Data

It is the network monitoring and network maintenance data to guarantee the network operation, including network configuration data, alarm data, real-time performance monitoring data, and so on. Network configuration data, mainly refers to the configuration of the network equipment, including equipment, machine box, physical configuration data for the board, ports, and logic configuration data, as well as parameters of equipments, etc. The amount of network configuration data is relatively small, but it contains complex relationships, and the fulfillment process and network maintenance operations will change it frequently. Alarm data are the messages produced by network due to a variety of network faults. The active alarms are those alarms which hadn't been processed. The amount of active alarms is relatively small, but the active alarms need being accessed, transformed and processed rapidly. The performance data is those indicators that reflect the quality of the network operation. The examples of the performance data are CPU usage, call completing rate, SMS Successful send rate, SMS amount etc. The performance data is the guarantee normal operation of the network. The amount of performance data is relatively small also. All the 3 kinds of data can be processed with traditional data processing technologies.

The basis of real-time data is the Network configuration data because every piece of alarm data and performance data are related to one network configuration object. Because of that, the real-time data is structural and complex, and its amount is ten-million to hundred-million levels. The real-time data is generally stored in RDBMS to be processed in real time. Considering cost and scale of storage devices, the history alarm data and history performance data can be stored a part of most recent period.

3.2 Converging Data for Analysis

This kind of data contains the summary analysis results or intermediate results which refer to the real-time data above, and those source data retrieved from other systems for data mining such as network fault analysis, alarm analysis and network resource analysis etc. The converging data for analysis provides data support for network data, network quality improvement optimization and management decision-making. This kind of data mainly is the structural, its real-time demand is not high, and its amount is big, generally use the data warehouse for processing.

3.3 Usage Data

This kind of data is those data which produced by the network when users enjoy the telecommunication services. It records that users how, where, and when use telecommunication network in details. The examples of the usage data include the DPIs, CDRs, AAA bills, DNS logs, WAP bills which are used for multi-dimension statistic and analysis and service using detail query. The usage data is collected directly from network devices and is transformed into regular format, stored in files. The usage data mostly are structural but contains a few relationships. Due to big population of users of China Telecom, the data volume growth of the usage data is very fast, about hundreds of Trillion bytes per day. Those characteristics of the usage data lead to that it cannot be processed with traditional data processing technologies. Only distributed data storage technology and concurrent computation technology to meet the requirements of collecting quickly, processing in time. The usage data is the real big data in the INMS, and how to process is the central issue of this thesis. The big data processing functions in the INMS include data loading, cleaning, conversion, associated, gathering, statistics, analysis, and there are higher performance requirements in analysis results showing, and detail data querying.

4 The Big Data Processing Project in INM Platform

4.1 INMS Data Center Overall Technical Framework

Network Operation Data Center is the core component of the INM platform, the basic framework as shown in Fig. 2:

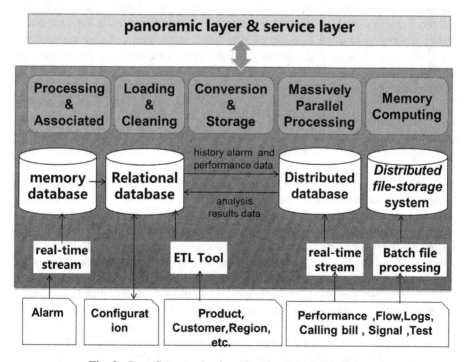

Fig. 2. Data Center technology framework in INM platform

In all kinds of data acquisition, pretreatment must be done. For the alarm data, After being processing by the real-time streaming processing components, they can be rapidly sent into the memory database for interface showing, and sent into the relational database for data persistence simultaneously. Resource configuration data collection directly into a relational database, data required for other systems, use ETL tools to load. For performance, data flow, log, calling bill, signal log, test data, have done a certain degree of analysis and data format standardization work through the underlying network, which also generates data files for being collected by the INM platform. For those data files which have small size, large data access frequency and high real-time demand, using real-time streaming technique is used to send them into the treasury; For other data files, batch processing technique is used to load them into the distributed file system.

INM platform Data Center, is mainly responsible for data loading, extraction, transformation, storage, cleaning, and calculation. For huge amounts of data, need to use massive parallel computing to meet the performance requirements for dealing with data. For real-time requirements of data processing for memory computing technology. Through the Data Center for data processing, supporting the upper-layer analysis of a variety of applications, such as network quality analysis, user perception analysis, etc.

4.2   The Analysis of the Technology of Data Processing

Big data itself is a phenomenon rather than a technology. It is accompanied by big data collection, transmission, processing and application of related techniques are the big data processing technology. It uses a series of non-traditional tools for distributed parallel processing of large amounts of structured, semi-structured and unstructured data to obtain the results of the analysis and prediction of a series of data processing technology.

We have to consider the storage, processing and application of big data. Cloud-based distributed architecture can support big data storage and processing requirements. Due to the low cost of hardware, software, and operations, more economical and practical, and that makes it possiblefor big data processing and using. The use of big data processing technology, will help people to manage large data storage and extraction of value from large volume, high complex data.

For big data in INM platform, generally refers to all types of data for analysis, including resource data, alarm history data, network performance data and user networks and services produced by a variety of details of a single data which will be with the network continuing operations and continue to rapidly increase. After analyzing the existing big data processing technology, data processing technology for INM platform, mainly uses the Hadoop framework, for the results of data processing, metadata management and basic data, are stored in a relational database.

China Telecom's network performance data is more complex, mainly structured data. For a relatively strong correlation and update more data, use a relational database for data processing. For the massive data storage, computing, analysis technology, and use the Hadoop framework for processing, and statistical analysis of the results, stored in a relational database, and further analysis of data at any time convenient to show.

4.3   Hadoop-Based Mass Data Processing Architecture

According to the characteristics of Hadoop and the requirement for massive data processing INM platform, China Telecom INM platform based on the data of the technical framework of Hadoop processing architecture is shown in Fig. 3:

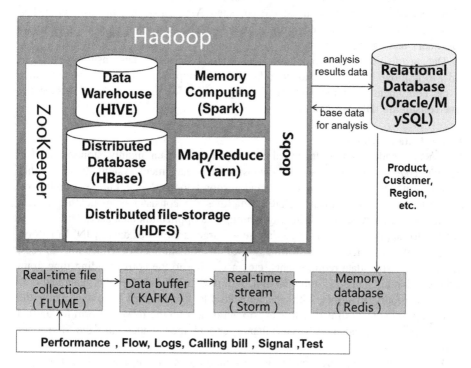

Fig. 3. Hadoop-based big data processing architecture

Massive data processing mainly uses Hadoop mature technology framework and a variety of components for maritime data collection, storage, computing, import, export and other applications, to provide fast and convenient data needed for upper-layer analysis.

4.3.1   Data Collection and Pretreatment

Operational and performance data used in INM platform in business, after all formatted files and logs stored in a distributed manner on the respective acquisition machine, you can use Cloudera Flume to carry huge amounts of data in real-time file collection. As the speed of data acquisition and data processing is not necessarily synchronized, so the need to add a messaging middleware as a buffer, can be used to achieve the Apache KAFKA. The traditional collection network on the details of a single data file, use the FTP mode, to improve the efficiency of the collection through the use of multiple threads, after collecting the data, you can use the PUT command, the data directly loaded into the HDFS store.

Due to the different collection way of files are generated, size to differ, in order to improve the hadoop for data processing speed, before loading to the HDFS, to merge the data file, the smaller files, merge into the size of 64 MB of files, and partition storage by region and date.

For the collected data to some pre-processing, use Storm stream processing technology to improve processing speed, and can be the basis of some static data memory database Redis associate, such as: the collected AAA bills, and the user base data further action can be associated terminal base data, and then put in storage, to facilitate post query and aggregation, etc.

Data acquisition, pretreatment and loaded into HDFS, is a time-consuming work. In order to improve the speed of loading data into Hadoop, according to the performance of the equipment is divided into a plurality of job for processing, and reduce the time-consuming data association.

4.3.2   Data Storage

After using hadoop-based technical architecture, the data mainly store in HDFS. Hadoop HDFS is the basis of the data storage management system. It is a highly fault-tolerant system that can detect and respond to hardware failure, running on low-cost commodity hardware. HDFS simplifies the consistency model file, access through the data stream, providing high throughput application data access function, is suitable for applications with large data sets. Large amounts of data in INM platform are currently collected in file format, based on the number of collection devices, network size, size, data requirements, etc., according to the corresponding time grain (typically 1 min, 5 min, 15 min, 30 min, 1 h, day, month, etc.) of the generated data files in appropriate format with standardized file names, then save them into the provincial or date sub-directory to store, to get data from the INM platform for unified acquisition module adapted to each harvester and then loaded into the HDFS for storage.

For the HDFS data, after cleaning, association, conversion, then inserted into the HBase self-built a variety of data in the table. HBase is in the Hadoop ecosystem storage details of a single database, query speed, linear expansion and other characteristics, can better meet the requirement for mass storage and fast query demand of INMS. For Statistical analysis mass data which have less real-time demand, can use the Hive data warehouse for data mining analysis framework.

4.3.3   Data Calculation

Based on the data stored in HDFS, you can use M/R for distributed computing, Hadoop's automatic scheduling of computing tasks, is very convenient in programming. INM platform uses the Yarn version of the product to calculate, through programming, realize the diversification and deep processing of data. In order to improve the efficiency of data calculation, Spark can be used in memory computing. Due to the merger of the data file, the file number is greatly reduced, the file size is more appropriate, can significantly improve the processing speed of Map/Reduce.

4.3.4   Data Import/Export

Intermediate data or analysis summary data in the INMS, are loaded into relational database by using Sqoop component of Hadoop for facilitating further analysis and query to. Meanwhile, some basic data, such as: user data, resource data, etc., in order to carry out the analysis of data association, will be loaded synchronously into the Hive or HBase by Sqoop.

5 Application Effect of Big Data Processing in INMS

China Telecom INM platform and application deployed in resource pool of Inner Mongolia cloud base,has now collected the DPI data, CDR data, AAA bills, WAP bills, DNS logs, from whole network of China Telecom. These data centrally stored in the INMS Network Operation Data Center, and be used to construct some effective and practical analysis application.

The following is the big data applications of several typical practice:

(1) Use of DPI data to analyze mobile Internet user behavior, analyzing various application characteristics code to find user habits preferences and accurate users demand, analyzing the quality of business to enhance the user perception and user maintain relationship, collecting classification of instant hot information Automatically and integrate high-quality resources to enhance the 3G user activity for different users requirement.

(2) Based on user home location and user visitor location information in signaling data to analyze the personnel traffic and flow direction in key areas, and provide timely and accurate basis data for the government and the tourism sector.

(3) User perception analysis, based on massive user voice and Internet data, customer complaints data, DT/CQT data, multi-dimensional data modeling, depth mining, intelligent correlation analysis and supplemented by expert experience, to achieve the user experience evaluation objectively, and solve the Inconsistent of performance metrics and user perception. This analysis has greatly enhanced efficiency of user complaints processing, timely and comprehensive present regional network problems, verified the effect of construction and maintenance optimization automatically and accurately.

(4) The application has found and optimized network regional issues automatically based on user perception analysis. According associated analysis with the wireless multi-dimensional data, change network optimization personnel work pattern, strengthen the execution of basis network optimization standard, and automatic tracking network optimization effect, then reducing the workload of DT/CQT.

Using the big data processing technology, complete the DPI and CDR data analysis application that the traditional way is difficult to do, The query speed is significantly faster than before, the time range of data statistical analysis is more from a few week before to a year now, even more. Based on the results of big data applications the analysis, play an important role in fault location network maintenance, network optimization and expansion, Precise marketing, active service customer. Based on big data processing platform in the Network Operation Data Center, Will do more deeper analysis application, to meet the all analysis requirements.

6 Future and Prospects

At present, China Telecom set up a team for INMS operations, Data Center operations is the most important part of. Operations team is collecting the entire network through the INM platform running production of data, data-rich core assets of China Telecom, based on analysis of these data is made, has just begun, massive data processing techniques, there are many needs optimize the sound aspect. INMS is the core of the future of China Telecom's network management systems, the Network Operations Data Center is the core of the future in INMS, in order to further good use data assets and maximize the value of INMS, but also need to learn to Internet companies to improve data intelligent analysis model, increase the depth and breadth of large data processing applications. With the further improvement of the INMS data and big data processing technology to mature, and large data processing technology and the application of network data center operations, you will get better value development, the value of data, intelligent network management applications, will be further demonstrated.

References

1. 周平利,王燕川等,"集约化运营下智能网管体系规划研究",《电信科学》, 6 (2014)
2. 周宝曜、刘伟等,《大数据:战略·技术·实践》,电子工业出版社,(2013年)
3. White, T.: Hadoop: The Definitive Guide. 2nd (edn) (2011)

Estimating the Missing Traffic Speeds via Continuous Conditional Random Fields

Bing Liang[1]([✉]), Chong Chen[1], Ying-Hui Guan[1], and Xiao-Yu Huang[2]

[1] Academy of Guangdong Telecom Co. Ltd., Guangzhou 510630, China
Jiangb@gsta.com
[2] School of Economics and Commerce,
South China University of Technology, Guangzhou 510006, China

Abstract. Recently, increasing interests have been emerging in the data driven intelligent transportation systems [27], some typical applications include flock pattern recognition, road network structure inference and route searching. However, almost all the applications suffer from the missing data problem. In this paper, we propose to adopt the Continuous Conditional Random Fields (CCRFs) model [24] to estimate the missing historical traffic data. We exam the proposed method with a real traffic speed dataset, results show that it is superior to the comparison algorithms.

Keywords: Continuous conditional random fields · Missing data · Sequence estimation · Intelligent transportation systems

1 Introduction

Recent advances of the Intelligent Transportation System (ITS) have witnessed the popularity of the traffic speed data based transportation applications, examples include online real time traffic information services [1,8,16], road network structure inference [5,6,9], periodic traffic behavior recognition [7,21], congestion pattern extraction [4,12] and dynamic routing services [3,11,17]. However, almost for all these applications, suffer from the data missing problem more or less [20,27]. Addressed to this problem, in the present work we study to impute the missing data with the following settings: Let $R \in \mathbb{R}^{n \times m}$ be a matrix consisting of the mean traffic speed values of n urban roads (within the same city) in m consecutive time frames, where $R_{i,j}$ is the value of road i in frame j, but if there were no data collected throughout j, then we say the value of $R_{i,j}$ is *missing*, and denote as $R_{i,j} = `\perp`$. With the representation above, our focus is to estimate all the missing values of R.

Our main tool is the Continuous Conditional Random Fields (CCRFs) model [24], we make the choice mainly for two reasons: Firstly, as will be shown in later discussion, based on the analysis of a large scale real traffic speed dataset, we find that the missing entries of R always occur in consecutive time moments, i.e., for an arbitrary road i, if $R_{i,j} = `\perp`$, then for a relatively large k, it's

© Springer International Publishing Switzerland 2015
R. Cai et al. (Eds.): APWeb 2015 Workshops, LNCS 9461, pp. 35–43, 2015.
DOI: 10.1007/978-3-319-28121-6_4

most likely that the equation $R_{i,j+l} = `\perp'$ holds for the all l with $1 \leq l \leq k$, too. So instead of estimating the independent missing *point* values, the problem in front of us is to estimate the missing *sequence* values. Secondly, as a variant of the Conditional Random Fields (CRFs) model [19], CCRFs does not only inherit all the superior sequence estimating capacity from CRFs, but also have the extended ability to perform inference on the real values, so it's worthy of desire to achieve success in our problem.

The organization of the paper is as follow: In Sect. 2 we review related works, in Sect. 3 we proceed the analysis of the traffic data with a real data set, in Sect. 4 we present the estimation algorithm. Section 5 is devoted to the empirical analysis, and Sect. 6 is the conclusions.

2 Related Works

2.1 Missing Traffic Data Imputation

In principle, works on the missing traffic data imputation problem can be classified into three categories: The neighborhood model, the regression model and the subspace model.

The neighborhood model is based on the observations that the traffic condition of an arbitrary road r at any time moment t is always close to the condition of r at $t + 1$, as well as the conditions of the adjacent roads of r at t. As the result, for every entry with missing values, the neighborhood model simply imputes it with the mean (or weighted sum) of the traffic data that collected in the same road at neighbor time moments, or in the adjacent roads at the same time, or both of the above [10,23]. Despite of its simplicity, the neighborhood model often works very well, but existing empirical studies also show that when the observed data are rare, the model will inevitably suffer from the accumulate estimation error problem, hence it's not suitable for long missing sequence inference problem.

In the regression model, the missing traffic values are often estimated in a *road-by-road* scheme. For each road whose values to be predicted (i.e., the target road), the regression model treats the values of the road as the responses, while the values of the other roads as the variables. The model proceeds the predictions in two stages: in the first stage, it fits a linear mapping f from the variables to the responses w.r.t. the values observed in the target road; in the second stage, it apply f to predict the missing values of the target road w.r.t. the corresponding variables. Many efforts have been devoted into various regression models, examples including [2,18,26]. The main drawback of the regression model is, in the model, the road network structure information is simply disregarded, while which should have benefitted for the predictions.

The subspace model often adopts a matrix representation for the traffic data, just as our settings, where every row corresponds to a road and every column corresponds to a time moment. The basic assumption of the subspace model is the data matrix is spanned by a small set of basis (row or column) vectors, so to make the prediction, it first decomposes the (incomplete) traffic matrix into the product of two low rank submatrices — one as the basis matrix and the other as the coefficient matrix — with respect to the non-missing data; then the missing values are approximated by the corresponding ones in the product. Empirical studies have shown the promising performance of the subspace model, and some recent proposed subspace models can also proceed with some structural prior information [14,15], but it still remains hard to incorporate some more complex information, e.g., the road network structure, to work.

2.2 Conditional Random Fields (CRFs) and Continuous Conditional Random Fields (CCRFs)

The CRFs model was proposed by Lafferty et al. [19]. Given the observations X and random variables Y, let $G = (V, E)$ be a graph such that $Y = (Y_v)_{v \in V}$, so that Y is indexed by the vertices of G. Then (X, Y) are a conditional random fields when the random variables Y_v, conditioned on X, obey the Markov property with respect to G, i.e.,

$$p(Y_v | X, Y_w, w \neq v) = p(Y_v | X, Y_w, w \sim v),$$

where $w \sim v$ means that w and v are neighbors in G.

In other words, CRFs are an undirected graphical model where the nodes are divided into two disjoint sets X and Y, X are the observed nodes (or, observations) and Y are the latent nodes (or, labels), respectively, and the conditional distribution $p(Y|X)$ is then modeled.

Ever since its proposition, CRFs have been widely employed into various sequence learning problems, such as text parsing [25], image labeling [13], trace analysis [22], etc. And it has also yielded state-of-the-art performance in most of the tasks. However, concerning the conventional CRFs, one of its main drawbacks is it can only predict the *discrete* variables, while there are still many tasks that need to forecast the *continuous* variable sequences, e.g., time series predictions. Addressed to the limitation, Qin et al. proposed the continuous conditional random fields (CCRFs) model [24], where the target sequence can be composed by any real numbers.

Given the observation X, to derive the target (real number) sequence Y, in CRFs (as well as CCRFs), Y is defined as the solution to the following conditional probability:

$$Y^* = \underset{Y}{argmax} Pr(Y|X)$$

where

$$Pr(Y|X) = \frac{1}{Z(X)} exp\{-\sum_j \sum_p \alpha_p h_p(y_j, X) - \sum_C \sum_q \beta_C g_q(Y_C, X)\} \quad (1)$$

In Eq. (1), the subscript j is used to index the sequence elements, C is to index the max cliques of Y, the terms $h_p(y_j, X)$ and $g_q(Y_C, X)$ are feature functions, Z is the normalized factor, which is defined as

$$Z(X) = \int_Y exp\{-\sum_j \sum_p \alpha_p h_p(y_j, X) - \sum_C \sum_q \beta_C g_q(Y_C, X)\} dY.$$

To ensure $Z(X)$ integrable, we restrict that $\alpha_p > 0$ and $\beta_q > 0$ for all α and β.

3   Data Analysis and Notations

Throughout this paper we proceed the analysis with a traffic speed dataset collected by the GPS devices from Zhuhai city, China. As mentioned above, all the data are stored in a matrix R with $n(= 6194)$ rows and $m(= 15840)$ columns, where n is the number of roads and m is the number of the consecutive 5 min time frames. We use $R_{i,j}$ to denote the mean traffic speed of road i in frame j, but if no speed values were collected in j, we denote $R_{i,j} = `\perp$'.

Our initial statistics shows that in R there are only about 8 million non-missing values, noting that the total number of entries in R is nearly 100 million, hence the missing ratio is 92 %. Besides, we also find that the number of non-mergeable blank sequences is about 1.4 million(here a *blank sequence* refers to a row sequence consisting of only '$\perp$' values, if the union of two blank sequences is also a blank one, then we say they are mergeable, and vice versa), noting that the number of the '$\perp$' values is about 92 million, so we have the immediate result that the average length of a blank sequence is 65, or in other words, the average blank time length is about 5.5 h. Based on the observations, it's clear that rather than to predict the independent missing point values, we are more likely need to predict the missing long sequence values.

The main notations we use in the paper are summarized in Table 1.

Table 1. Summarization of the notations.

Notation	Description
n	Number of rows of R
m	Number of columns of R
$R_{i,:}$	The ith row of R
$R_{:,j}$	The jth column of R
$R_{i_1:i_2,j_1:j_2}$	A sub-matrix T of R, where $T \in \mathbb{R}^{(i_2-i_1+1)\times(j_2-j_1+1)}$ and $T_{i,j} = R_{i_1-i+1,j_1-j+1}$
$R_{i,-j}$	A row vector v with length $m-1$, where $v_l = R_{i,l}$ for $1 \le l < j$, and $v_l = R_{i,l+1}$ for $j \le l < m$
$R_{-i,j}$	A column vector v with length $n-1$, where $v_l = R_{l,j}$ for $1 \le l < i$, and $v_l = R_{l+1,j}$ for $i \le l < n$
$R_{-i,:}$	A sub-matrix of R which is composed by all rows of R except $R_{i,:}$
$R_{:,-j}$	A sub-matrix of R which is composed by all columns of R except $R_{:,j}$
$R_i^{s:t}$	The row sequence $< R_{i,s}, R_{i,s+1}, \ldots, R_{i,t} >$
$\hat{x}$	The estimation of variable x, where x can be either a single value (e.g., $R_{i,j}$) or a sequence value (e.g., $R_i^{s:t}$)

4 The Proposed Approach

Given the (incomplete) speed matrix R, for any $1 \leq i \leq n$ and $1 \leq s < t \leq m$, we define the optimum estimation for a sequence $R_i^{s:t}$ as follow:

$$\hat{R}_i^{s:t} = \underset{S \in \mathbb{R}^{t-s+1}}{\arg\max} Pr(S|R_{-i,s:t}) \tag{2}$$

We assume the data of R have the conditional linear chain dependent structure, as illustrated in Fig. 1.

observations

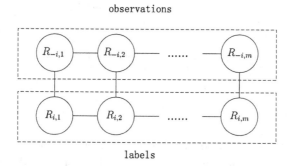

labels

Fig. 1. The non-null values ratio of the roads

In Fig. 1, we employ the undirected solid lines to describe the probabilistic dependency among the data. It's seen where the matrix $R_{-i,:}$ is treated as the set of observations, and the jth value of $R_{i,:}$ (i.e., $R_{i,j}$) as the label of $R_{-i,j}$, hence the solution to Eq. (2) is also the optimum label sequence for $R_{-i,:}$ w.r.t. the column vectors. Noting that Fig. 1 is exactly as the same as the linear structured CCRFs, as the result, the term $Pr(S|R)$ of Eq. (2) instantializes Eq. (1) as follow:

$$Pr(S|R_{-i,s:t}) = \frac{1}{Z(R_{-i,s:t})} exp\{-\sum_{l=s}^{t}\sum_{p} \alpha_p h_p(S_l, R_{-i,s:t}) - \sum_{l=s}^{t-1}\sum_{q} \beta_q g_q(S_l, S_{l+1}, R_{-i,s:t})\} \tag{3}$$

where S_l is the lth element of S, $Z(R_{-i,s:t})$ is the normalization factor.

Below we present our design policy for the feature functions $h_p(\cdot, \cdot)$ and $g_q(\cdot, \cdot)$.

First, we note that in Eq. (3), S_l and S_{l+1} represent the traffic speeds of the same road in neighbor time moments, respectively, since the interval between the two moments is small, we simply let $q \in 1$, $\beta_q = 1$ and define

$$g_q(S_l, S_{l+1}, R_{-i,s:t}) = (S_l - S_{l+1})^2 \tag{4}$$

As to $h_p(S_l, R_{-i,s:t})$, similar to $g_q(\cdot, \cdot)$, our idea is make use of the speed information of the non-target roads at time l to help the prediction, for simplicity, we let $p \in \{1\}$ and define

$$h_p(S_l, R_{-i,s:t}) = \sum_{j \neq i} s_{i,j}(S_l - R_{j,l})^2 \qquad (5)$$

where we use $s_{i,j}$ to measure the *closeness* between road i and j, specifically, $s_{i,j} = 1$ if i and j are adjacent, and $s_{i,j} = 0$ if they aren't.

Another issue we need to address is on the missing data. We note that in Eq. (5), besides of S_l, the value of $R_{j,l}$ can be missing, too. Taking this observation into consideration, we need to fix Eq. (5) slightly, as follow:

$$h_p(S_l, R_{-i,s:t}) = \frac{\sum_{j \neq i} \mathbb{I}(R_{j,l} \neq `\perp' \wedge Adj(i,j))(S_l - R_{j,l})^2}{\sum_{j \neq i} \mathbb{I}(R_{j,l} \neq `\perp' \wedge Adj(i,j))} \qquad (6)$$

Where the function $Adj(i,j)$ indicates whether the roads i and j are adjacent or not, if *Yes*, then it returns *true*, else it returns *false*.

5   Experiments

Below we present the evaluation results of our proposed model, as well as the those attained by the comparison algorithms, all the experiments are performed on the Zhuhai City traffic speed dataset.

5.1   The Settings

Since the experiment dataset is highly incomplete, for evaluation, we only select the top 300 roads (or, the rows of R) with the most observations to consist the experiment set, where each road has at least 50 % non-missing values.

We randomly select 30 roads from the experiment dataset to consist the test set, while all the others form the training set. For each test road, we only keep 50 % of the (randomly chosen) observations for training, while the other 50 % is left for testing.

We employ the root square mean error (RMSE) as the accuracy measure, given a set of variables $x_1, x_2, \ldots, x_k$, denote the estimations as $\hat{x}_1, \hat{x}_2, \ldots, \hat{x}_k$, then the estimated error is:

$$RMSE(x_1, x_2, \ldots, x_k; \hat{x}_1, \hat{x}_2, \ldots, \hat{x}_k) = \sqrt{\frac{\sum_{s=1}^k (x_s - \hat{x}_s)^2}{k}}$$

As to the detailed settings of our model, we employ Eqs. (4) and (6) as the implementations of g_p and h_q of Eq. (3), respectively. Besides, we set the all αs and βs of Eq. (3) to be 1.

Table 2. Results of comparison studies.

	SW	MAFED	CCRFs
RMSE	8.81	7.31	7.12

5.2   The Results

In this section we report the empirical results of comparison studies. The benchmark algorithms we used are the sliding window (SW) and MAFED [15], where the former is a classical local model, while the latter is a recent proposed global method. The results are presented in Table 2.

From Table 2 we see our proposed CCRFs model outperforms both of the comparison models, as to the reasons, concerning SW, we think it's mainly because that SW only cares the speed information of the same road, while all the traffic information of the other roads are disregarded; for the MAFED model, though it's global, it can only interplay with the road network structure implicitly, compared with CCRFs, the latter does better in making full use of the spatial information.

6   Conclusions

In this paper, we study the missing traffic speed estimation problem. We first formulate the problem as to label the sequence composed by the non-target roads' speed values, with the representation, we can apply continuous conditional random fields (CCRFs), the powerful sequence learning model, to the imputation problem. We perform empirical studies on the proposed method as well as the benchmark algorithms, all the experiments are conducted with real traffic dataset, the results show that our method is superior to the others.

Acknowledgments. The research was partially supported by the National High Technology Research and Development Program (863) of China (NO. 2012AA12A203).

References

1. Google Map. https://maps.google.com/, visited May 2015
2. Al-Deek, H., Venkata, C., Chandra, S.R.: New algorithms for filtering and imputation of real-time and archived dual-loop detector data in I-4 data warehouse. Transp. Res. Rec. J. Transp. Res. Board **1867**(1), 116–126 (2004)
3. Andersson, M., Gudmundsson, J., Laube, P., Wolle, T.: Reporting leaders and followers among trajectories of moving point objects. Geoinformatica **12**(4), 497–528 (2008)
4. Benkert, M., Gudmundsson, J., Hübner, F., Wolle, T.: Reporting flock patterns. Comput. Geom. Theory Appl. **41**(3), 111–125 (2008)

5. Bruntrup, R., Edelkamp, S., Jabbar, S., Scholz, B.: Incremental map generation with gps traces. In: Proceedings of Intelligent Transportation Systems, pp. 574–579. IEEE (2005)

6. Cao L., Krumm, J.: From GPS traces to a routable road map. In: Proceedings of the 17th ACM SIGSPATIAL International Conference on Advances in Geographic Information Systems, pp. 3–12. ACM (2009)

7. Elfeky, M.G., Aref, W.G., Elmagarmid, A.K.: Periodicity detection in time series databases. IEEE Trans. Knowl. Data Eng. **17**(7), 875–887 (2005)

8. Fan, R.C., Yang, X., Fay, J.D.: Using location data to determine traffic information, 15 July 2003. US Patent 6,594,576

9. Fathi, A., Krumm, J.: Detecting road intersections from GPS traces. In: Fabrikant, S.I., Reichenbacher, T., van Kreveld, M., Schlieder, C. (eds.) GIScience 2010. LNCS, vol. 6292, pp. 56–69. Springer, Heidelberg (2010)

10. Gold, D.L., Turner, S.M., Gajewski, B.J., Spiegelman, C.: Imputing missing values in ITS data archives for intervals under 5 minutes. Presented at the 80th Annual Meeting of the Transportation Research Board, Washington, DC (2000)

11. Gonzalez, H., Han, J., Li, X., Myslinska, M., Sondag, J.P.: Adaptive fastest path computation on a road network: a traffic mining approach. In: Proceedings of the 33rd International Conference on Very Large Data Bases, VLDB 2007, pp. 794–805. VLDB Endowment (2007)

12. Gudmundsson, J., van Kreveld, M.: Computing longest duration flocks in trajectory data. In: Proceedings of the 14th Annual ACM International Symposium on Advances in Geographic Information Systems, GIS 2006, pp. 35–42. ACM, New York (2006)

13. He, X., Zemel, R.S., Carreira-Perpindn, M.: Multiscale conditional random fields for image labeling. In: Proceedings of the 2004 IEEE Computer Society Conference on Computer Vision and Pattern Recognition, CVPR 2004, vol. 2, p. II-695. IEEE (2004)

14. Huang, X.-Y., Li, W., Chen, K., Xiang, X.-H., Pan, R., Li, L., Cai, W.-X.: Multimatrices factorization with application to missing sensor data imputation. Sensors **13**(11), 15172–15186 (2013)

15. Huang, X.-Y., Xiang, X.-H., Li, W., Chen, K., Cai, W.-X., Li, L.: Matrix factorization for evolution data. Math. Probl. Eng. **2014** (2014)

16. Huber, W., Lädke, M., Ogger, R.: Extended floating-car data for the acquisition of traffic information. In: Proceedings of the 6th World Congress on Intelligent Transport Systems, pp. 1–9 (1999)

17. Kanoulas, E., Du, Y., Xia, T., Zhang, D.: Finding fastest paths on a road network with speed patterns. In: Proceedings of the 22nd International Conference on Data Engineering, ICDE 2006, p. 10. IEEE Computer Society, Washington (2006)

18. Kwon, T.M.: TMC traffic data automation for Mn/DOT's traffic monitoring program. Technical report MN/RC-2004-29, Minnesota Department of Transportation (2004)

19. Lafferty, J.D., McCallum, A., Pereira, F.C.N.: Conditional random fields: probabilistic models for segmenting and labeling sequence data. In: Proceedings of the Eighteenth International Conference on Machine Learning, ICML 2001, pp. 282–289. Morgan Kaufmann Publishers Inc., San Francisco (2001)

20. Li, L., Li, Y., Li, Z.: Efficient missing data imputing for traffic flow by considering temporal and spatial dependence. Transp. Res. Part C: Emerg. Technol. **34**, 108–120 (2013)

21. Li, Z., Ding, B., Han, J., Kays, R., Nye, P.: Mining periodic behaviors for moving objects. In: Proceedings of the 16th ACM SIGKDD International Conference on Knowledge Discovery and Data Mining, KDD 2010, pp. 1099–1108. ACM, New York (2010)

22. Liao, L., Fox, D., Kautz, H.: Extracting places and activities from gps traces using hierarchical conditional random fields. Int. J. Rob. Res. **26**(1), 119–134 (2007)

23. Nguyen, L.N., Scherer, W.T.: Imputation techniques to account for missing data in support of intelligent transportation systems applications.Technical report UVACTS-13-0-78, University of Virginia, Center for Transportation Studies (2003)

24. Qin, T., Liu, T.-Y., Zhang, X.-D., Wang, D.-S., Li, H.: Global ranking using continuous conditional random fields. In: Advances in Neural Information Processing Systems, pp. 1281–1288 (2009)

25. Sha, F., Pereira, F.: Shallow parsing with conditional random fields. In: Proceedings of the 2003 Conference of the North American Chapter of the Association for Computational Linguistics on Human Language Technology, vol. 1, pp. 134–141. Association for Computational Linguistics (2003)

26. Shuai, M., Xie, K., Pu, W., Song, G., Ma, X.: An online approach based on locally weighted learning for short-term traffic flow prediction. In: Proceedings of the 16th ACM SIGSPATIAL International Conference on Advances in Geographic Information Systems, GIS 2008, pp. 45:1–45:4. ACM, New York (2008)

27. Zhang, J., Wang, F.-Y., Wang, K., Lin, W.-H., Xu, X., Chen, C.: Data-driven intelligent transportation systems: a survey. IEEE Trans. Intell. Transp. Syst. **12**(4), 1624–1639 (2011)

GPU-Based Parallel Processing Technology in DPI

Zhimin Zhong[✉], Yuliang Zhang,
Guanglong Yang, and Yongping Kong

Guangzhou Research Institute of China Telecom Co. Ltd., Guangzhou, China
{zhongzm, zhangyl, yangguangl, kongyp}@gsta.com

Abstract. This paper mainly discusses the design, implementation and performance test of GPU-based parallel processing technology in deep packet inspection (DPI) field, which is used for building high-speed network traffic processing applications using low-cost hardware. Meanwhile topics in the paper include principles of GPU parallel computing, and how they're applied in pattern matching, signature inspection, state inspection, self-learning, multi-classification and some other aspects.

Keywords: DPI · GPU · GPGPU · Parallel computing

1 Introduction

New mobile internet applications are emerging explosively in recent years, such as stream media, Peer-to-Peer service, VoIP, IPTV, multimedia instant message, interactive online games and virtual reality and so on. The application protocols are increasing and changing continuously at the same time. With the information explosion, the traffic jam problems are getting worse and there're great impacts on the network bottom flow and upper application model, also lead to new requirements like bandwidth management, content billing, information security, etc.

Deep Packet Inspection (DPI) technologies come into being at the right moment. Protocol detection is more and more difficult with the increasing of mobile Internet bandwidth and applications. 40G or even 100G bandwidth gradually become the mainstream in backbone network. However, high-speed packet inspection technology is still at the stage of 10G–20G bandwidth processing ability. The high cost of DPI equipment is one of the mayor reason that hinder large-scale deployment. The emergence of commodity many-core architectures, such as multi-core CPUs and modern graphics processors (GPUs) has proven to be a good solution for accelerating many network applications, and has led to their successful deployment in high-speed environments. This paper is focusing on the GPU-based parallel detection technology, which can significantly improve the throughput and recognition ability with single equipment, and reduce the equipment cost at the same time. As a result, the throughput of single equipment can meet the requirements from 40G to even 100G bandwidth.

R. Cai et al. (Eds.): APWeb 2015 Workshops, LNCS 9461, pp. 44–53, 2015.
DOI: 10.1007/978-3-319-28121-6_5

2 Development of GPU-Based Parallel Computing Technology

GPU (Graphic Processing Unit), which widely used in computers, game consoles, mobile phones and other multimedia equipment, is responsible for the processing of graphics tasks. Before the invention of GPU, computer graphic processing operations were performed by CPU (Central Processing Unit). The GPU and CPU architectures varied a lot to achieve different goals. CPU has many function modules and can adapt to the complex computing environment, is suitable for completing a task as quick as possible. Most transistors in CPU are used for the construction of control circuit and cache, only a small part of transistors are performing computation. Different from CPU, the main task of GPU is calculating and building the image of millions of pixels (parallel processing of millions of task). The control function and architecture of GPU is relatively simple therefore. Majority of transistors in GPU are flow processors and memory controllers, which have more powerful parallel processing ability.

With the improvement of computing speed, the introduction of stream processing, high intensive parallel computing, programmable pipeline and other new technical features, greatly raise the processing capabilities and expand the application range of GPU. As GPU has the efficient parallel and flexible programming features, it's used fulfilling some non-graphic rendering calculations by more and more researchers and business organizations, and initiates a new field of research: General-Purpose computation on GPU (GPGPU) [1], which is about how to use GPU for more extensive scientific computing besides graphics processing.

CPU and GPU heterogeneous mode is a common architecture in GPGPU, in which CPU is responsible for complex logic processing and transaction processing and those non-parallel computing task while GPU is responsible for intensive parallel computing of large-scale data. Powerful processing ability and high bandwidth of GPU make up the performance of CPU, and has significant advantages in developing computer potential performances. Before the launch of NVIDIA's CUDA (Compute Unified Device Architecture) in 2007 [2], development of GPU general computing is quite difficult because of the hardware programming and development mode constraints. Since the development of CUDA, several other GPU general-purpose computing standards have been put forward, such as OpenCL, stream SDK (by AMD), and Direct Compute (by Microsoft), etc. Applications can be easily ported on GPU using these languages.

In CUDA programming model, CPU plays the role of Host and GPU as the Device. There could be one host and several devices in one system commonly. CPU and GPU have independent memory spaces: host memory and device graphics memory. CUDA memory operations are basically the same with C, while a new pinned-memory is added. What different is operations on graphics memory in CUDA need to call API memory management functions. Once the parallel part of the program is identified, the computation of this part can be done using GPU. The CUDA parallel computation function running on GPU is called kernel function. A complete CUDA program is composed of a series of parallel kernel function steps on device side, and the serial processing steps on host side. These processing steps are executed sequentially according to the corresponding sentences order in program.

3 The Development of DPI Technologies

DPI technology is the core technology of network intrusion detection and application layer protocol identification. It plays an increasingly important role in the field of network and information security. By analyzing the five-tuple array or seven-tuple array information (increase the input and output interface index information), to subdivide the different types of applications, especially those don't depend on five-tuple or seven-tuple information become very difficult. Different from those traditional technologies, DPI is in-depth restructuring, analyzing the seventh layer payload contents and use service feature-matching, to identify the service and application types.

There're some specific inspection methods in DPI technology, such as payload signature matching, interactive service identification, behavior pattern identification and flow statistics identification technology and so on.

Payload Signature Matching Technology: It identifies the applications of service flow by matching the data packet payload signatures. Four sub-branch technologies are as following: fixed (or variable) position signature matching, multi connection joint matching and status signature matching technology. Payload signature matching technology can be easily extended to the detection of new protocols by upgrading of signature database. Fixed position signature matching is the simplest way.

Interactive Service Identification Technology: At present, VoIP/FTP/online games and some other services are interacting with the control flow separation from the service flow, control flow handshaking take charge of negotiating the service flow port number. By using DPI technology, control flow protocols need to be analyzed first, and then identify the service flow to find out the port of service flow or the gateway address.

Behavior Pattern Identification Technology: The terminal behavior identification model should be established firstly, then based on which, the behavior pattern identification technology can judge the action taking or going to be implemented according to the behaviors that the user implemented before. This technology is usually used on the service that is difficult to be determined by protocols solely.

Flow Statistics Identification Technology: Based on the data flow behavior signature, the service or application type could be distinguished by comparing with the data model of application flow that already built. With this principle, the behavior signature index is matched with inspection model, such as the connection number of various applications, the connection mode of single IP address, the proportional relationship of upstream and downstream, transmitting frequency of the data packet, then, the application type could be distinguished.

As a conclusion, there are three key points in DPI technology methods. (1) Multi-pattern keyword inspection technology. (2) Multi-pattern regular inspection technology. (3) Packet signature learning and statistical technology. Most of the DPI devices are using these three technologies. Effectively integrated using these three technologies is a critical issue to improve the efficiency of DPI.

4   Integrated Using of CPU and GPU Technology

When using GPU technology in DPI, there are several key issues, including Data transmission, Pattern matching, Signature computation and Packet sampling, etc.

4.1   DPI System Architecture Based on GPU and CPU

There are three layers in system: data layer, exchange layer and control layer, as Fig. 1 shows.

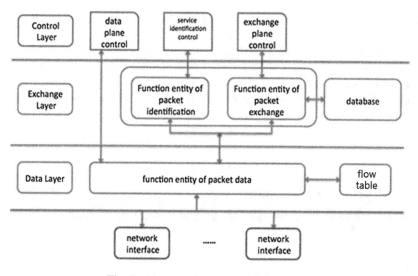

Fig. 1.   The overall structure of the system

The packet acquisition and sending according to flow-control table is completed in data layer. Unrecognized flows are identified in exchange layer, where the identified protocol type are added to the flow-control table. The following packets will be routed according to the corresponding routing instruction in the flow-control table. Control layer take charge of the data layer and exchange layer service control through protocols such as openflow or sflow. The packet identification function entity is completed by GPU independently.

Packet identification process is as Fig. 2.

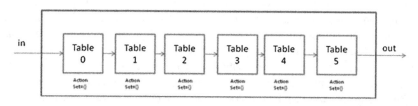

Fig. 2.   Packet identification process

Each packet after entering the system would be looked up in the flow-control table to decide whether it belongs to a known protocol. If the packet protocol could not be identified, then sent to the packet identification entity that is the DPI identification module. Then the new protocol will be added into the flow-control table after that identification. The table is a multi-stage cascade control entity. Users can define route controlling commands in the table based on protocol number, source IP, destination IP, port number and VLAN, etc.

4.2   Task Collaboration Between GPU and CPU

The computing unit of CPU is thread and process, while GPU's basic computing unit is flow processor. Data are transferred between CPU and GPU via PCI-E bus. The bandwidth of PCI-E 3.0 is as high as 32 GB/s, which is fast enough meeting the need of DPI computation. Packet contents transferred from the host to GPU are expressed in three vectors: content vector, index vector and flow vector. However contents from the GPU to the host includes flow vector only. The index vector and the content vector don't return to the host. Figure 3 shows the task collaboration schema.

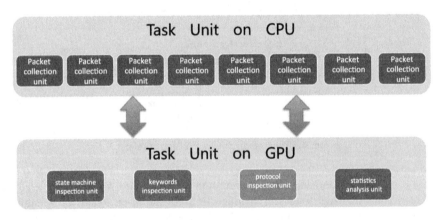

Fig. 3. Task Collaboration between GPU and CPU

The key point of the task collaboration is to integrate different technologies using parallel computing framework, so as to maximize each unit's capability and improve the overall performance of the system.

The tasks of each flow processor in GPU include: packet sampling, signature computing and probability statistics. The first two take the packet and the third takes flow as the basic computing unit. The first step, a flow processor takes a packet, samples it, and saves the result in an intermediate vector. The second step, according to the existing models, computes the probability of each signature with the feature vector. The final step, according to the feature vector corresponding to each flow, calculates the probabilities sum-up of a matched protocol, and give out the highest possible protocol number. The internal processing flow of GPU is shown as Fig. 4.

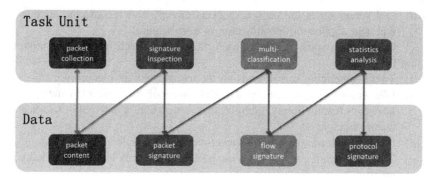

Fig. 4. Internal processing flow of GPU

The following methods is conducted in packet signature sampling:

- Keyword sampling.
- For HTTP protocol, HOST and USER-AGENGT are sampling values.
- For SSL protocol, the certificate ID and DOMAIN are extracted as sampling values.
- Histogram sampling of the packet's first 16 bytes and the last 16 bytes.
- Character density sampling of the packet's first 64 bytes and the last 64 bytes.

We made a GPU-based DPI performance evaluation.

(a) Test Environment:

- Traffic-generating server:
  - NUMA nodes (Intel Xeon E5520 2.27 GHz quad-core CPUs)
  - 2 × 16 GB DDR3 1066 MHz RAM
  - 2 × Intel 82599 EB network adapters (with dual 10 GbE ports)
  - Ubuntu 12.04 Linux
- DPI server:
  - NUMA nodes (Intel Xeon E5520 2.27 GHz quad-core CPUs)
  - 2 × 16 GB DDR3 1066 MHz RAM
  - 2 × Intel 82599 EB network adapters (with dual 10 GbE ports)
  - 1 × NVIDIA GTX780 graphics cards
  - Ubuntu 12.04 Linux

(b) Test Data:

- 20 types of large, 512 types of small network packets, such as IM, P2P, MAIL, VOIP, Video and so on.
- Total packets size is 15 GB.

(c) Training Process:
  (i) Calibrate each training packet and identify the application type and application ID of the packet flow.
  (ii) Put all training data into the training list.

(iii) DPI server reads the training packets directly and records the application type and application identification of each feature.

(iv) Output the associated data of each protocol and each feature after training.

(d) Test Process:

(i) Traffic-generating server loads all the test packets into memory.

(ii) DPI server loads the associated model library of the application and features, keywords feature library, multi-regular feature library and multi-classification feature library.

(iii) DPI server loads the DPDK packet-receiving module.

(iv) Traffic-generating server sends the packets in memory to DPI server in cyclic order.

(v) DPI Server receives the packets and dispatches GPU to identify them.

(vi) Output the corresponding five-tuple and protocol identification of each flow.

(e) Test Result:

GPU has a great advantage of its large number of flow processors. So a good design of the computation units is the key to parallel computation. We use packet and flow as basic computation units, and collect 8 loaded packets from each flow, every packet can be turned into a feature vector. Then, after computing the signature probability density of the 8 feature vectors, we can get the similarity between the flow and the setup model (Table 1).

CPU mainly completes the functions like flow management, packet collection, packet control, QoS and so on. Each core of CPU corresponds to a thread of flow management, responsible for the creation and aging of the flow. Four flow management threads correspond to one GPU processing thread. Each GPU processing thread can handle 800,000 packets per second, which correspond to 100,000 flows according to our packet sampling rules. In general, 10Gbps responds to 50,000 to 100,000 new flows that respond to 1/2–1 GPU processing capability, and the current server architecture supports 2 or 4 GPUs. So a single server can achieve the parallel processing capability of 40 Gbps by extending GPUs.

4.3   Key Technologies

Implementation of GPU-Based AC Algorithm. The AC inspection technology is efficient for keyword inspection. AC multi-pattern matching algorithm is based on finite state automata (FSA) and KMP prefix algorithm. The algorithm guarantees that, given a text of length n and a pattern set P {P1, P2, ... Pm}, all the target patterns in the text can be found in time complexity of $O(n)$, independent of the size m of the pattern set.

We adjust the AC algorithm by using the perfect hash algorithm to store the goto table of keywords, and realize the linear storage of sparse values. It improves the detection speed, while saves the storage space at the same time. Our test results show that the matching time of 100,000 packets with 100,000 pattern strings is only 5–10 ms.

Table 1. GPU-based DPI performance evaluation test result

	1	2	3	4	5	6	7	Average
Length of the data sent to GPU for processing (Byte)	12,533,332	14,464,240	12,472,646	11,794,784	11,222,842	8,087,516	11,222,842	11,685,457
Amount of the packets sent to GPU	21,904	20,524	20,603	21,385	20,530	21,514	20,530	20,999
Transmission time of GPU to CPU (ms)	0.002752	0.005888	0.001984	0.002592	0.005792	0.001792	0.005792	0.0038
Duration of sampling (ms)	20.09482	20.49996	19.909808	15.511948	19.917492	14.248604	19.917492	18.5857
Duration of the flow computation (ms)	6.4806	6.9467	6.6477	6.3771	6.4906	7.1635	6.4906	6.6567
Average data processing capability (Gbps)								3.7
Average packet processing capability (/ms)								831.8

GPU-Based DFA Inspection Algorithm. Multi-pattern regular inspection technology is used widely in the inspection of non-fixed keywords and the extraction of the packet information. The DPI engine based on regular expressions is constructed by transforming the regular state machine to NFA or DFA. An NFA is easy to construct but the matching speed is lower than the equivalent DFA that needs more spaces. So we transform the regular expressions to NFA and then transform NFA to DFA. The DFA constructing time is relatively longer but the regular expressions only need to be compiled once before matching, so the matching speed is much faster than that of NFA. We transplant the DFA based multi-pattern inspection algorithm to GPU [3]. In our test the matching time of 100,000 packets with 100,000 regular string is 10–20 ms. It's very suitable for floating pattern string comparison and protocol field extraction.

Packet Identification Algorithm Based on Statistics. Statistical Protocol Identification (SPID) algorithm is mainly for pattern learning of packet multiple signatures [4]. It constructs the attributes probability matrix in the learning phase. The typical features include length of the first packet in upstream, length of that in downstream, the first character of the first packet load in upstream and that in downstream. It then uses the probability matrix to match protocols in the inspection phase, and get the protocol that best matches by calculating the matching degree. Figure 5 shows the basic procedure.

The computing unit of SPID inspection technology is flow. This algorithm can effectively improve the identification of new protocols by learning methods. However, under traditional CPU computing architecture, when the matrix extended or protocol

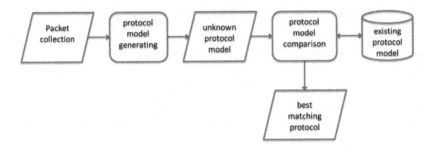

Fig. 5. Flow model of SPID algorithm

quantity increased, the computation complexity increases constantly. This problem can be solved effectively by using GPU. At present, based on GPU parallel computing, in a model with 256 attributes matrix and 1024 protocols, the inspection time of 10,000 flows only needs 10–20 ms.

The above three inspection technologies, utilizing GPU parallel computing on the basis of traditional algorithms, can shorten the packet inspection time effectively, improve the packets throughput, combine the packet inspection technology with the flow inspection technology, and greatly improve the packet identification efficiency. At the same time, when new protocols appear, these technologies can learn the new models faster.

Packet Collection Technology Based on Intel® DPDK. Another factor that affects the speed of DPI identification is packet sending and receiving speed, as is network data processing speed. Intel DPDK uses UIO, HUGEPAGE and CPU Affinity technologies to improve the processing performance of high-speed network data [5]. In our test, with the help of DPDK, a single Intel Xeon processor can provide more than 80 Mpps throughput.

5 Summary

At present, the application of GPU in DPI mainly focus on accelerating the key modules by GPU parallel computing to improve computing speed, such as pattern matching, matrix computation, Fourier transform and so on. GPU can also be used in speech recognition, image recognition, data mining and analysis, such as KMeans acceleration, EM acceleration, GMM acceleration and so on. In the near future, GPU will be applied to more general purpose computing applications.

References

1. GPGPU [EB/OL]. http://www.gpgpu.org
2. NVIDIA CUDA [EB/OL]. http://developer.nvidia.com/object/cuda.html

3. Liu, C.H., Hon, W.K., Chang, S.C., et al.: PFAC library: GPU-based string matching algorithm (2012)
4. Hjelmvik, E.: The SPID algorithm-statistical protocol identification. Gävle, Sweden, October 2008
5. Intel DPDK vSwitch, Getting Started Guide, December 2013

Mining the Discriminative Word Sets for Bag-of-Words Model Based on Distributional Similarity Graph

Wen Wen[(✉)], Zhifeng Hao, and Ruichu Cai

School of Computer, Guangdong University of Technology, Guangdong, China
wwen@gdut.edu.cn

Abstract. Most of the previous distributional clustering methods are fundamentally unsupervised, and the discriminative property of words is not well modeled in the clustering procedure. In this paper, we propose a supervised model which involves the class conditional probability in measuring the word similarity, and transform the word-set extraction to a supervised graph-partition optimization model. A greedy algorithm is proposed to solve this model, which combines the word selecting method and the word grouping method in the unified framework. By grouping the related words, this method essentially transforms the exact match between word bins to fuzzy match between groups of related-word bins, which to some extent avoid the synonymous problems in BoW model. Experiments on data sets demonstrate that the proposed method is applicable for both text sets and image sets, and has advantages in producing better retrieval precision and meanwhile reducing the lexicon size.

1 Introduction

Bag-of-Words model (BoW) is a widely-used model in natural language processing [1], computer vision [2, 3] and information retrieval [4]. The basic ingredient of BoW is to represent the text or images as the bag of its words, and the frequency of each word is used as the feature for classification or retrieval. Although the BoW model has been demonstrated to be successfully applied in many fields, it is still a big challenge for categorization or retrieval in the cases of high-dimensional lexicon. In this case, sparse distribution of words makes it difficult for the classifier or retrieval engine to catch the discriminative characteristic of samples. A lot of works have been done to reduce the "words" in the BoW model. For example, mutual information (MI), information gain (IG) and Chi squared statistics are used to measure the influence of text words on category label, and words with high influential weights are selected [5]. MI and IG are also used for eliminating stop words or other unimportant words for the BoW model in computer vision [6]. However, the above methods are based on eliminating words that is unimportant. They do not solve the problem that some words might be inherently related with each other.

Since BoW model fundamentally disregards grammar and semantic relationship between words, polysemy and synonymy is widely found in both text data and image data. And this has been demonstrated to influence the categorization or retrieval

R. Cai et al. (Eds.): APWeb 2015 Workshops, LNCS 9461, pp. 54–70, 2015.
DOI: 10.1007/978-3-319-28121-6_6

precision [7]. There have been several methods aiming to eliminate the negative effect of BoW model. One kind of methods are to find the relationship between words based on the prior determined semantic networks, such as Wordnet [8, 9], a lexical database built for English language, and rule-based feature-relation network, a word-relation network generated by rule-based method [10]. In this kind of methods, semantic distance between words is calculated using the information in predefined or pre-generated word-network. However, such methods highly depend on the predefined lexical database or rules, which demand expertized knowledge and are problem-specific.

It has been demonstrated that related words tend to have similar statistical characteristics, in both text data [11] and image data [2, 12–14]. Therefore, some researchers proposed to model and extract the underlying relationship among different words based on their statistical distribution. For example, Pereira et al. [13] proposed to use distributional clustering for grouping English words. But this method relies on an iteratively-annealing algorithm, and different annealing parameters yield different hierarchical "soft" clustering of the data, which reduces the plausibility of this algorithm. Slonim and his colleagues proposed a revised version of distributional clustering [12], which iteratively cluster the documents based on clustering the words. This method is also implemented to find visual phrases for computer vision in 2007 [15]. However, since it is fundamentally an unsupervised method, the discriminative property of words is not modeled in the clustering procedure, which make it not guarantee to find the best groups of words for classification or retrieval. To explore the use of statistical property of the distribution of words in classification and retrieval is still an important issue.

In this paper, we propose to model the relationship among words based on a distributional similarity graph. The similarity between two words is measured using Jensen-Shannon divergence, and then words with close similarity value are iteratively grouped. Words in the same group are used as a higher-level "concept" for retrieval. Meanwhile the whole grouping procedure is guided by the retrieval precision, which guarantees achieving better discriminative property. The contribution of this paper is that we demonstrate probabilistic relation can be effectively utilized in BoW model for both texts and images, and can be used to group related words for better discriminative property. This paper is organized as follows: Sect. 2 presents related works on feature extraction and selection for BoW model. The proposed method is given in Sect. 3. Section 4 consists of detailed experiments and in-depth discussions. And the conclusion is drawn in Sect. 5.

2 Related Woks

In this section, we concentrate on the related works for modeling or extracting discriminative features for BoW model. As mentioned above, polysemy and synonym are two important problems widely found in both images and texts. And ambiguity of words has been realized ever since the BoW model is proposed [7]. Some scientists focus on clarify the semantic meaning of words in BoW model, and suggest to reduce the ambiguity of words by manually labeling the items with appropriate semantic labels [9]. For example, researchers in the field of natural language processing propose to model the relatedness of concepts using Wordnet [8, 16], and experts in computer vision propose to manually label the semantics of visual words for categorization [17]. Such manually-handling methods require comprehensive consideration of the semantic relationship among words in BoW model, which is somewhat an implausible task in many cases.

Other methods based on the modification of traditional cosine similarity measures are also proposed. For example, Earth mover's distance (EMD), an intuitive distance metric for comparing two histograms is used as the metric for image retrieval [18, 19]. EMD allows flexible cross-bins measurements. However, in traditional EMD, ground distance is fixed and predefined, which requires prior knowledge on the relationship between words [19]. Some other researchers proposed to use supervised EMD [7] for measuring the similarity between word histograms. In supervised EMD, the ground distance between two bins is learned and adaptively determined using the information from labeled pairs. Cross-bins relationship is then adaptively adjusted and reflected in the learned ground distance of visual words. To some extent, supervised EMD can find underlying relationship between words. But the whole algorithm is guided by the precision of labeled pairs, which ignores the statistical information. And since it demands iterative adjustment of the weights, which needs high computational complexity, it is impossible to be implemented in the cases of large quantity of visual words. Except for the methods based on EMD, methods based on the soft assignment of word in the matching stage are also proposed [20]. These methods use probabilistic word voting scheme to reduce the intra-ambiguity of words. That is, word primitives are considered belonging to multiple high-level concepts. When comparing the frequency histogram of BoW, closer neighbors in the same concepts are weighted heavier than further ones [21]. This method requires good assignment of word's weights, which is usually a difficult and implausible procedure.

It has been found that inherent related words have similar statistical distribution property in both the cases of text data [5, 13, 22] and image data [6, 14]. Therefore, another important category of methods based on the statistical analysis of word co-occurrences are proposed. Distributional clustering is one of such methods. Class conditional distribution is considered as an important criterion for characterizing the statistical property of words. This method is based on the assumption that intra-related words probably have high similar class conditional probability. Pereira et al. proposed a hierarchical distributional clustering method to find groups of synonyms in English words [13]. And in 2008, Zheng et al. proposed to use the Information Bottleneck (IB) clustering procedure for finding the visual synsets of images [14], which adopted sequential IB clustering algorithm [22]. This method finds local optimal partition of original visual word sets (which is called lexicons in 22) through minimizing the objective function

$$L[P(S|C)] = I(S;C) - \beta I(V;S) \tag{1}$$

However, this method requires quite high computational complexity and it is difficult to determine the parameters: cluster number K and the balanced parameter β.

In this paper, we ignore the low-level difference between text words and visual words, but just focus on the statistical distributional property of words, and aim to model and extract the discriminative features based on BoW model. We try to find the inherent relationship between words based the probability distribution and propose a method similar to the distributional clustering, but differing from the sequential distributional clustering in the initializing stage and iterative grouping procedure. Meanwhile, we include the consideration of a flexible stop criterion, such as retrieval precision, in the clustering procedure, which makes it easier to determine the parameters of the algorithm.

3 The Proposed Method

Although it is obvious that the low-level characteristics are different between text words and visual words, it has been demonstrated that some common statistical properties are found in both of them. One is that both the distribution of visual words and text words on their corresponding corpus satisfies Zipf laws [6]. Another is that the conditional probability distributions tend to be similar for inherent related words. For example, it is found in English words that different words which describe the same concept tends to have quite similar class distributions [12, 13], so does visual words corresponding to the same instance [14].

In this paper, the lexicon is denoted by $\Omega = \{w_1, w_2, \ldots, w_T\}$, which totally contains T visual words. The item w_t in the lexicon is corresponding to a visual word. Given a set of labeled samples, which is denoted by $S = \{S_1, S_2, \ldots, S_n\}$. These samples are classified into C categories and the ith sample is represented by the vector $S_i = \{f_i(w_1), f_i(w_2), \ldots, f_i(w_T)\}$, here $f_i(w_t)$ is the occurrence frequency of word w_t in sample S_t, which defined as formula (2).

$$f_i(w_t) = n(w_t|s_i) \tag{2}$$

Here, $n(W_t|S_i)$ is the occurrence frequency of w_t in the sample S_t. Cosine similarity between the frequency vectors of two samples is used as the retrieval metric, and samples with high similarity values are returned as the retrieval results.

The major objective of this paper is to find the inherent related words, and group them to produce discriminative concepts for text or image retrieval. This is based on three important parts. One is to reasonably model the extracting procedure. Another is to appropriately measure the underlying relationship of words. And the third is to find an appropriate algorithm for solving the proposed model and extracting the discriminative word sets. All of the three parts are discussed in the following.

3.1 Supervised Grouping Model for BoW

We model the extracting procedure as a process to find the appropriate partition of a weighted network. Generally, the network is based on the similarity distance among the distributions of visual words. Vertices in the graph represent words and edges between two nodes represent the underlying relationship between two distributions. The mathematical formulation of the graph is defined as follows.

$$G = \langle V, E, g_v(V), g_e(E) \rangle \tag{3}$$

$$E\{e_{s,t}|s = 1, \ldots T; t = 1, \ldots, T\} \tag{4}$$

$$V = \{w_t | t = 1, \ldots, T\} \tag{5}$$

$$g_v(w_t) = P(C|w_t), t = 1, \ldots, T \tag{6}$$

$$g_e(e_{s,t}) = d(w_s, w_t), s = 1, \ldots, T; t = 1, \ldots, T \tag{7}$$

Here, G denotes the similarity graph, E is the set of edges in G, and V is the set of vertices of G. g_v is the weighting function of vertices and g_e is the similarity weight function of edges. G is initialized as a complete graph, which contains exactly one edge between each pair of distinct vertices. The objective of our method is to find the useful words in the original lexicon, and group the most related words to improve the retrieval precision. This is transformed to a supervised graph partition optimization problem.

Given a p-partition of the graph denoted by

$$\pi_p = \{V_1, \ldots V_p\}, \cup_{i=1}^{p} V_i \subseteq V, V_i \cap V_j = \phi, \forall i \neq j. \tag{8}$$

Each subset V_i is related to a group of words, which can be viewed as the description of a given concept. The problem of finding groups of words is transformed to computing the following representation from the input samples,

$$\varphi = (p, \pi_p). \tag{9}$$

And our objective is to select and group related words for better retrieval. Top-K precision is used here as the criterion for retrieval quality, therefore the supervised word grouping naturally becomes an optimization problem maximizing top-K precision in the solution space Φ.

Denote the similarity of samples defined on a given partition of word-graph by

$$SIM_\varphi(s_i, s_j), i = 1, 2, \ldots, n, j = 1, 2, \ldots, n \tag{10}$$

In this paper, Cosine similarity is used to calculate $SIM_\varphi(s_i, s_j)$.

The top-K retrieval precision for the ith sample can be formulated as

$$Prec@K(i; \varphi) = \sum_{j=1}^{K} \delta\left(s_i, \arg_{s_j}\left(SIM_\varphi(s_i, s_j)\right)_{j:n}\right)/K \tag{11}$$

where $(SIM_\varphi(s_i, s_j))_{1:n} \leq \cdots \leq (SIM_\varphi(s_i, s_j))_{n:n}$ are the ordered similarity between the ith sample and the others. And $\delta(s_i, s_j)$ is an indicator function defined as

$$\delta(s_i, s_j) = \begin{cases} 1, & \text{if } s_j \text{ is the correct retrieval result of } s_i \\ 0, & \text{if } s_j \text{ is the correct retrieval result of } s_i \end{cases} \tag{12}$$

Thus the objective function becomes

$$max_{\varphi \in \Phi} \sum_i Prec@K(i; \varphi) \tag{13}$$

The solution space

$$\Phi = \left\{ \varphi = (\pi_p, p) | \pi_p = \{V_1, \ldots V_p\} \bigcup_{i=1}^p V_i \subseteq V, V_i \cap V_j = \phi, \forall i \neq j; p = 1, \ldots, T \right\} \tag{14}$$

consists of exponential number of feasible solutions. Therefore the optimization problem is obviously NP-hard. In the following section, we will present the detailed information about the edge weight and a greedy algorithm which produces local optimal solutions for the above model.

3.2 Distributional Similarity Among Words

An important ingredient of the above model is the measurement of the statistical similarity between words, which relates to the edge weights in formula (7). Here, a symmetric distributional similarity is used. C denotes the random variable over class. Thus given a particular word w_t, the class distribution can be written as $P(C|w_t)$. Given another word w_s, the corresponding class distribution is $P(C|w_s)$. The distance between $P(C|w_t)$ and $P(C|w_s)$ is used as a metric reflecting the semantic relationship between w_t and w_s. K-L divergence is widely used to measure the distance between two distributions [6], which is defined as follows.

$$D_{KL}(P(C|w_t) \parallel P(C|w_s)) = \sum_{j=1}^{|C|} P(c_j|w_t) log \left(\frac{P(C_j|w_t)}{P(C_j|w_s)} \right) \tag{15}$$

One technical difficulty is that $D(P(C|w_t) \parallel P(C|w_s))$ is not defined when $P(C|w_s) = 0$ but $P(C|w_t) > 0$. The traditional method sidesteps this problem by smoothing zero frequency using a very small real number. However, since there are some circumstances that the data is quite sparse, which make the measure not reliable.

In this paper, we use a revised version of Jenen-Shannon (JS) divergence defined as formula (16) for measuring the relationship between two words.

$$d(w_s, w_t) = (p(w_t) + (w_s))D_{JS}(P(C|w_t) \parallel P(C|w_s)) \tag{16}$$

Here,

$$D_{JS}(P(C|w_t)) \parallel P(C|w_s)) \triangleq P(w_t) * D_{KL}(P(C|w_t)\bar{P}) + P(w_s) * D_{KL}(P(C|w_s) \parallel \bar{P}) \tag{17}$$

$$\bar{P} \triangleq \frac{P(w_t)}{P(w_t) + P(w_s)} P(P(C|w_t)) + \frac{P(w_s)}{P(w_t) + P(w_s)} P(P(C|w_s)) \tag{18}$$

This distance is chosen for it has several good properties. Firstly, this distance is symmetric, which is more suitable for measuring the relationship between two words. Besides, it avoids directly computing the KL divergence between two individual visual words, but between a word distribution and the average distribution $\bar{P}$, which makes the distance still reliable even in the case of zero frequency of some words. Last, but certainly not least, according to [9], the proposed distance is demonstrated to be the estimation of the decrease of mutual information after merging w_s and w_t.

3.3   A Greedy Algorithm for the Supervised Word-Grouping Model

To solve the proposed model in Sect. 3.2, a kind of greedy algorithm is proposed, which guarantees the value of objective function does not decrease in each step. The framework of the proposed greedy algorithm is illustrated as Fig. 1. The algorithm contains two modules: selecting module and grouping module. In the selecting module, "important" or "necessary" words are selected from the original lexicon. In the grouping module, related words are tentatively grouped in order to produce better representation. Each module can be implemented independently, or combined to generating better solutions.

Fundamentally, the selecting module and the grouping module can be respectively viewed as a special case of the solution for the optimizing problem (formula (13)). That is, the selecting module gives the solution that each selected word is considered an isolated sub-graph,

$$\pi_p = \{V_1, \ldots, V_P\}, V_i = \left\{w_i'\right\}, \bigcup_{i=1}^P V_i \subset V, \forall i \neq j. \tag{19}$$

And the grouping module gives the solution of dividing the original lexicon into different groups of words, without eliminating redundant words, that is

$$\pi_p = \{V_1, \ldots, V_P\}, \bigcup_{i=1}^P V_i = V, V_i \cap V_j = \phi, \forall i \neq j. \tag{20}$$

Since the number of feasible solutions is with exponential growth and the solution procedure a kind of greedy searching algorithm which requires repeated calculations, thus low computational complexity of the selecting module and grouping module is very important. Prior statistical information, such as mutual information, χ^2.statistics and the distributional weight of edges, is implemented for finding the better solutions. The detailed process of selecting module and grouping module is described as follows.

Selecting Module (SM)
Input: Sample vectors $s_i = \{f_i(w_t)|t = 1, \ldots, D\}, i = 1, \ldots, l$

- Calculate average statistics of each word according to formula (21)–(22) or (23)–(24)
- Sort the average statistics in ascending order

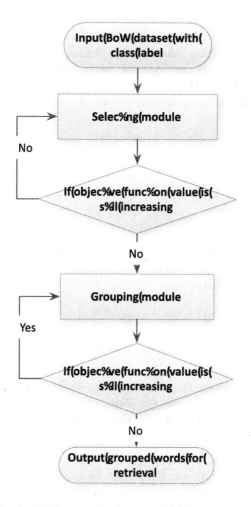

Fig. 1. The framework of the greedy solution algorithm

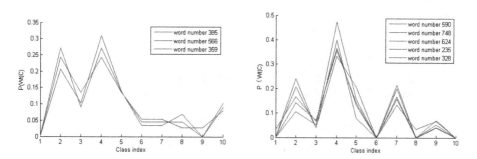

Fig. 2. Two groups of words found by MISM-GM on PI100 data set

- Do

  Eliminate words with 5 % lowest average statistics

  While the objective function value is still increasing

  Output: Sample vectors on optimal word subsets $s_i = \{f_i(w_t)|t = 1,$ $..., D^*\}, 1 = 1, ..., 1, D^* \leq D$

  Mutual Information of word items is defined as

$$MI(w_t, c_j) = log \frac{p(w_t, c_j)}{p(w_t) * p(c_j)} \tag{21}$$

And **the average MI** is defined as

$$MI_{avg}(w_t) = \sum\nolimits_{j=1}^{|C|} p(c_j) * MI(w_t, c_j) \tag{22}$$

χ^2 **statistics** [5] is defined as

$$\chi^2(w_t, c_j) = \frac{N * (freq(w_t, c_j) * freq(w_t, \neg c_j) - freq(\neg w_t, c_j) * freq(\neg w_t, \neg c_j))}{freq(c_j) * freq(\neg c_j) * freq(w_t) * freq(\neg w_t)} \tag{23}$$

Here, $freq(*)$ represents the frequency of a given word or class occurring in the data set. $freq(\neg c_j)$ represents the frequency that class c_j does not occur. $freq(\neg w_t)$ represents the frequency that w_t does not occur. And **the average χ^2** is defined as

$$\chi^2_{avg}(t) = \frac{1}{M} \sum\nolimits_{j=1}^{|C|} P(c_j) * \chi^2(w_t, c_j) \tag{24}$$

For convenience, in the following section **MISM** is short for selecting module using **mutual information** and **XXSM** is short for selecting module using χ^2 **statistics.**

Grouping Module (GM)

Input: Sample vectors $s_i = \{f_i(w_t)|t = 1, ..., D'\}; D' \leq D; i = 1, ..., n,$

Construct similarity graph

- Calculate node weights $P(c_j|W_t)$, $t = 1, ..., T; j = 1, ..., |c|$
- For $\forall s, t = 1, ...T, s < t$

  Calculate edge weights $d(W_s, W_t) = (p(W_t) + p(W_s))D_{JS}(P(C|w_t)) \parallel P(C|w_s)$

  (formulas (11) and (16)–(18))

Merge iteration

- Sort the edges in ascending order according to their weights $d(w_s, w_t)$
- Record the sorted edges as $d^{(1)}, d^{(2)}, ...d^{(|E|)}$, Here, $d^{(i)} = d\left(w_s^{(i)}, w_t^{(i)}\right), s < t$
- Initialize $i = 0$, and solution $\pi^{(0)} = \{V_1, ..., V_T\}, V_t = \{w_t\}$.

  (Each visual word is viewed as an isolated group in the initial stage)

  While the objective function value is still increasing

Scan the groups in $\pi^{(i)}$, merge groups contains words $w_s^{(i)}$ and $w_t^{(i)}$, and update $\pi^{(i)}$

$i = i + 1$

- End while

Output: Groups of words $\pi^* = \{V_1, \ldots, V_p\}$

What has to stress here is that the proposed algorithm is a kind of greedy method, which just guarantees finding local optimal solution. The advantage of this algorithm lies in that it can quickly select important words and find most related words according to their conditional probability. Actually, although both selecting module and grouping module can be carried out independently, according to our empirical experiments, it seems that "unimportant" words bring noises to the measurement of similarity among the words' distributions, which tends to influence the performance of grouping module. Therefore, in most cases, selecting module and grouping module are suggested to be combined for better solutions.

After finding the underlying related visual words as above, each word set is grouped as a "latent concept". Thus, the sample vector can be transformed to the word-group ("concept") vector. That is, each element in the sample vector corresponds with a group of words written as the formula (25):

$$s_i = \{f_i(V_1), f_i(V_2), \ldots, f_i(V_p)\} \tag{25}$$

Here, V_p represents a group of words that is found using the algorithm in Sect. 3.2, and

$$f_i(V_p) = \sum_{w_t \in V_p} n(w_t | s_i) \tag{26}$$

In the case of retrieval, the similarity between two samples is measured by the cosine distance between two transformed vectors as the above formula (26). And samples with top K similarity are returned to the users.

4 Experiments and Discussions

4.1 Datasets and Experimental Setup

Four real-world datasets are used to evaluate the proposed algorithm: two of them are image sets, and another two are text sets. The first image set is randomly selected from Product Image Categorization Data Set (PI100 dataset) [23][1], which totally contains 10 categories of product images and each category consists of about 120 images. Images in this data set are about single object or one dominant object, and do not contain complex background. We use sift features [24] as the visual primitives, and implement K-means clustering to generate a visual lexicon consists of 1024 visual words. The second image set is selected from Caltech256. To keep the variability of visual words, 30 categories are selected. And in each category, 30 images with dominant

---

[1] http://research.microsoft.com/en-us/people/xingx/pi100.aspx.

object (which make it more reliable to have visual semantics) are used for experiments. And sift features are used as the visual primitives, and a visual lexicon consists of 256 visual words is used for experiments.

Both of the two text sets are collected by a machine learning group of University of Maryland [25][2]: the webKB dataset and the citeseer data set are selected for experiments. The CiteSeer dataset consists of 3312 scientific publications classified into 6 classes. Each publication in the dataset is described by a 0/1-valued word vector indicating the absence/presence of the corresponding word from the dictionary. The dictionary consists of 3703 unique words. The WebKB dataset consists of 877 scientific publications classified into one of 5 classes. Each publication in the dataset is described by a 0/1-valued word vector indicating the absence/presence of the corresponding word from the dictionary. The dictionary consists of 1703 unique words.

In the experiments, all of the above data sets are split into two sets: 80 % of each category as the database set, and 20 % as the query set.

4.2 Experimental Results and Discussions

In order to evaluate the proposed method, we use Precision@K as the criterion to judge the validity of word-grouping procedure. Precision@K is defined to be the number of relevant documents in the top K positions given by a ranking, divided by K. Table 1 gives the results on four experimental datasets. The average retrieval precisions of target samples are respectively recorded as P@5, P@10 and P@15. It is demonstrated that for most of the four data sets the MISM-GM method produces the best retrieval precision. Besides, Table 1 also gives the compression rate of lexicon size of different solution methods. It is obvious that both the selecting module and grouping module produce reduced lexicon size. And the combination of selecting module and grouping module (MISM + GM and XXSM + GM) is able to further reduce the lexicon. This is means that the proposed greedy algorithm is able to keeping discriminative information in the grouped word sets, therefore can reduce the lexicon size while keeping high retrieval precision.

Figure 1 illustrates an example of two related groups of words produced by MISM-GM on PI100 data set. This gives an intuitive illustration that in the proposed method words with similar statistical property are grouped as the "latent concept". The most important is that, through grouping the related words, the proposed algorithm makes it possible to implements a kind of fuzzy match among related words: word by word match is transformed to word-set by word-set match. This is why the proposed method is able to produce the satisfactory results. Besides, Figs. 3, 4 and 5 illustrate some examples of word frequency histograms on reduced lexicon produced by MISM-GM and XXSM-GM. Word frequency histograms of image 1, image 3, and image 150 in PI100 data set are respectively presented in Figs. 3, 4 and 5. It is worth noting that Image 1 and image 3 in PI100 data set relates to the same object ('anklet'), but image 150 relates to different object ('baby_carriage'). It can be found intuitively in

---

[2] http://www.cs.umd.edu/~sen/lbc-proj/LBC.html.

Table 1. The precision results and reduced lexicon size

Data set		Method	P@5	P@10	P@15	Lexicon size	Compression rate
Image	PI100	Original word set	2.8737	5.3947	7.6368	1024	–
		MISM	2.9316	5.5105	7.7474	831	81.1 %
		MISM + GM	*3.0316*	*5.7105*	*8.1316*	754	73.6 %
		XXSM	2.8842	5.3579	7.7421	767	74.9 %
		XXSM + GM	3.2368	6.0112	8.6737	236	23.0 %
	Caltech256	Original word set	1.3429	2.2857	3.0714	256	–
		MISM	1.3429	2.2000	3.1143	255	99.6 %
		MISM + GM	*1.3429*	*2.3571*	*3.3571*	167	65.2 %
		XXSM	1.3429	2.2857	3.0714	255	99.6 %
		XXSM + GM	1.3429	2.3571	3.3571	167	65.2 %
Text	Citeseer	Original word set	2.7982	5.2534	7.6480	3703	–
		MISM	*2.9712*	5.7436	8.4006	3102	83.8 %
		MISM + GM	2.9530	*5.7481*	*8.4932*	2710	73.2 %
		XXSM	2.7982	5.3050	7.7360	2802	75.7 %
		XXSM + GM	2.8346	5.3657	7.8422	2212	59.7 %
	WebKB	Original word set	3.2431	6.3750	9.2431	1703	–
		MISM	3.6875	7.1250	10.5972	1254	73.6 %
		MISM + GM	*3.7500*	*7.5278*	*11.1250*	560	32.9 %
		XXSM	3.4583	6.6944	9.8125	1222	71.8 %
		XXSM + GM	3.5625	6.9028	9.9931	808	47.4 %

* Compression rate = (current lexicon size)/(original lexicon size)

Figs. 3, 4 and 5 that both MISM-GM and XXSM-GM seem to be able to produce the reduced lexicon which keeps similarity for images from the same category, and enlarge the difference between images from different categories, noting that cosine function is used here for measuring the similarity between two samples (Fig. 2).

For further analysis, if removing the stop criterion of the proposed greedy algorithm, the variation of precision as the change of dimension is illustrated in Figs. 6, 7, 8 and 9. Figure 6 illustrated detailed results of PI100 data set. Figure 7 relates to Caltech 256 data set. Figure 8 is about Citeseer dataset and Fig. 9 is for WebKB dataset. The horizontal coordinate in Figs. 6, 7, 8 and 9 represents the decrease of dimension, that is, "Original lexicon size-Dim(left)" represents the original lexicon size minus the current number of words or word sets. The vertical coordinate represent the variation of P@15. Figures 6, 7, 8 and 9 demonstrates that the proposed combination of SM and GM produces quite stable results on most of the four datasets. What should be emphasized here is that results in Table 2 and Figs. 6, 7, 8 and 9 also demonstrate the WE-WG can be used as a lexicon reduction method.

What should be noted here is that since the initial selected word sets are the same for both MISM + GM and XXSM + GM on Caltech256 dataset, the GM results are the same, which is plot overlapped in Fig. 7. In our experiments, it seems that for the four experimental data sets, low compression rate can be reached when keeping high

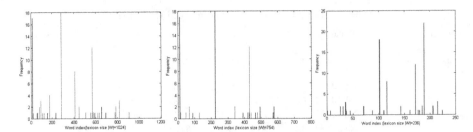

Fig. 3. Illustration of the word frequency on reduced lexicon produced by MISM + GM and XXSM + GM for image 1 in PI100. The Left, original lexicon size |W| = 1024; the middle, MISM + GM lexicon size |W| = 754; the right, XXSM + GM lexicon size = 236.

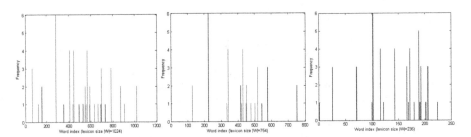

Fig. 4. Illustration of the word frequency on reduced lexicon produced by MISM + GM and XXSM + GM for image 5 in PI100. The Left, original lexicon size |W| = 1024; the middle, MISM + GM lexicon size |W| = 754; the right, XXSM + GM lexicon size = 236.

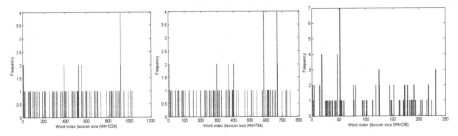

Fig. 5. Illustration of the word frequency on reduced lexicon produced by MISM + GM and XXSM + GM for image 150 in PI100. The Left, original lexicon size |W| = 1024; the middle, MISM + GM lexicon size |W| = 754; the right, XXSM + GM lexicon size = 236.

retrieval rate. This means that much fewer words or "concepts" is needed for retrieving or finding the target samples. This is a really interesting result.

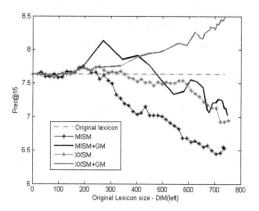

Fig. 6. Results on PI100 data set

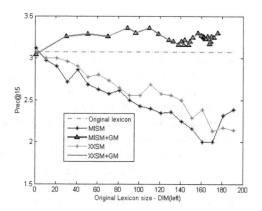

Fig. 7. Results on Caltech256 data set

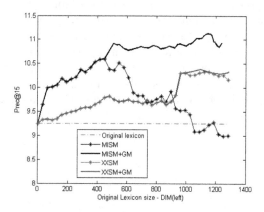

Fig. 8. Results on Citeseer data set

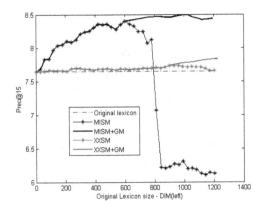

Fig. 9 Results on WebKB data set

5 Conclusions

In this paper, we reveal that through measuring the similarity among distributional probability of words, it is able to effectively extract the underlying related words for BoW model on both image data sets and text data sets. This implies that statistical property of words is a remarkable property in both images and texts. Experimental results have demonstrated that the proposed model and greedy algorithm has advantages in finding related words meanwhile keeping good retrieval precision. The proposed method is different from the previous distributional clustering method in the following points: firstly, the model is supervised, which involves the consideration of retrieval precision in the optimization objective. Secondly, other than measurement between words and the virtual cluster center in previous methods [11], the grouping module is based on direct measurement between two words. Thirdly, other than predefined the number of clusters, the proposed method is more flexible, in which number of word groups is determined by the user-defined criterion (for example, incremental retrieval precision in this paper). Last but not least, since it is to some extent a greedy method, which does not need to update similarity matrix in the grouping procedure, the proposed algorithm demands theoretically less computational complexity in each iteration, which makes it possible to be repeated for reaching an appropriate retrieval precision.

The method can be also extended to the cases of extracting phrases considering context information, and any other cases with the similar statistical property of features. Besides, the optimization objective can be substituted with other criterion, such as categorization precision, weighted precision, and et al. Therefore the proposed model has good flexibility.

References

1. Yogatama, D., Smith, N.: Making the most of bag of words: sentence regularization with alternating direction method of multipliers. In: Proceedings of the 31st International Conference on Machine Learning (ICML 2014), pp. 656–664 (2014)
2. Zhang, Y., Jia, Z., Chen, T.: Image retrieval with geometry-preserving visual phrases. In: Proceedings of the IEEE Conference on Computer Vision and Pattern Recognition (CVPR 2011), pp. 809–816 (2011)
3. Burghouts, G.J., Schutte, K.: Spatio-temporal layout of human actions for improved bag-of-words action detection. Pattern Recogn. Lett. **34**(15), 1861–1869 (2013)
4. Metzler, D.A., Jr.: Beyond bags of words: effectively modeling dependence and features in information retrieval. Dissertation, University of Massachusetts Amherst (2007)
5. Yang, Y., Pedersen, J.O.: A comparative study on feature selection in text categorization. In: Proceedings of the 14th International Conference on Machine Learning (ICML 1997), pp. 412–420 (1997)
6. Yang, J., Jiang, Y.G., Hauptmann, A.G., Ngo, C.W.: Evaluating bag-of-visual-words representations in scene classification. In: Proceedings of the International Workshop on Multimedia Information Retrieval, pp. 197–206. ACM (2007)
7. Wang, F., Guibas, L.J.: Supervised earth mover's distance learning and its computer vision applications. In: Fitzgibbon, A., Lazebnik, S., Perona, P., Sato, Y., Schmid, C. (eds.) ECCV 2012, Part I. LNCS, vol. 7572, pp. 442–455. Springer, Heidelberg (2012)
8. Budanitsky, A., Hirst, G.: Evaluating worldnet-based measures of lexical semantic relatedness. Comput. Linguist. **32**(1), 13–47 (2006)
9. Vogel, J., Schiele, B.: Semantic modeling of natural scenes for content-based image retrieval. Int. J. Comput. Vis. **72**(2), 133–157 (2007)
10. Abbasi, A., France, S., Zhang, Z., Chen, H.: Selecting attributes for sentiment classification using feature relation networks. IEEE Trans. Knowl. Data Eng. **23**(3), 447–462 (2011)
11. Baker, L.D., McCallum, A.K.: Distributional clustering of words for text classification. In: Proceedings of the 21st International ACM SIGIR Conference on Research and Development in Information Retrieval, pp. 96–103 (1998)
12. Slonim, N., Tishby, N.: Document clustering using word clusters via the information bottleneck method. In: Proceedings of the 23rd Annual International ACM SIGIR Conference on Research and Development in Information Retrieval, pp. 208–215. ACM (2000)
13. Pereira, F., Tishby, N., Lee, L.: Distributional clustering of English words. In: Proceedings of the 31st Annual Meeting on Association for Computational Linguistics, pp. 183–190 (1993)
14. Zheng, Y.T., Zhao, M., Neo, S.Y., Chua, T.S., Tian, Q.: Visual synset: towards a higher-level visual representation. In: IEEE Conference on Computer Vision and Pattern Recognition (CVPR 2008), pp. 1–8 (2008)
15. Yuan, J., Wu, Y., Yang, M.: Discovery of collocation patterns: from visual words to visual phrases. In: Proceeding of the IEEE Conference on Computer Vision and Pattern Recognition, (CVPR 2007) pp. 1–8 (2007)
16. Menéndez-Mora, R.E., Ichise, R.: Effect of semantic differences in wordnet-based similarity measures. In: Garcia-Pedrajas, N., Herrera, F., Fyfe, C., Benítez, J.M., Ali, M. (eds.) IEA/AIE 2010, Part II. LNCS, vol. 6097, pp. 545–554. Springer, Heidelberg (2010)
17. Mojsilović, A., Gomes, J., Rogowitz, B.: Semantic-friendly indexing and querying of images based on the extraction of the objective semantic cues. Int. J. Comput. Vis. **56**(1–2), 79–107 (2004)

18. Wan, X.: A novel document similarity measure based on earth mover's distance. Inf. Sci. **177**(18), 3718–3730 (2007)
19. Rubner, Y., Tomasi, C., Guibas, L.J.: The earth mover's distance as a metric for image retrieval. Int. J. Comput. Vis. **40**(2), 99–121 (2000)
20. Van Gemert, J.C., Veenman, C.J., Smeulders, A.W.M., Geusebroek, J.M.: Visual word ambiguity. IEEE Trans. Pattern Anal. Mach. Intell. **32**(7), 1271–1283 (2010)
21. Perronnin, F.: Universal and adapted vocabularies for generic visual categorization. IEEE Trans. Pattern Anal. Mach. Intell. **30**(7), 1243–1256 (2008)
22. Slonim, N., Friedman, N., Tishby, N.: Agglomerative multivariate information bottleneck. Advances in Neural Information Processing Systems, pp. 929–936 (2001)
23. Xie, X., Lu, L., Jia, M., Li, H., Seide, F., Ma, W.: Mobile search with multimodal queries. Proc. IEEE **96**(4), 589–601 (2008)
24. Lowe, D.G.: Distinctive image features from scale-invariant keypoints. Int. J. Comput. Vis. **60**(2), 91–110 (2004)
25. Sen, P., Getoor, L.: Link-based classification, University of Maryland Technical report CS-TR-4858 (2007)

Research of Botnet Situation Awareness Based on Big Data

Zhiqiang Luo$^{(\boxtimes)}$, Jun Shen, Huamin Jin, and Dongxin Liu

Guangzhou Research Institute of China Telecom Co. Ltd.,
109 West Zhongshan Ave, Tianhe District,
Guangzhou 510630, People's Republic of China
luozq@gsta.com

Abstract. With the rapid expansion of the botnet, a single network security system could not meet the requirement. Botnet situation awareness can dynamically reflect the overall botnet security and predict botnet security development trends. Characteristics of big data create opportunity for research breakthrough of large scale botnet situation awareness. This article discusses about botnet security situation awareness based on multi-source logs by utilizing big data analysis. It promotes detection accuracy and fast response of botnet events, and implements the early warning for DDoS attacks.

Keywords: Botnet · Big data · Situation awareness · Network security

1 Introduction

With cloud service's flourishing such as the Baidu cloud and the Alibaba cloud, the Internet has fully stepped into the cloud age. It is frustrating that the notorious botnet also adjusts itself into the cloud environment. Because of the powerful computing performance, huge available bandwidth and real-time online characteristics, a large number of hosts may be penetrated and turn into puppet machines by hackers in traditional data center or even in cloud data center. Thus, cloud service's great computing power and convenience could also provide some opportunity for cyber-attack, spamming, online fraud and etc.

Facing the menacing DDoS attacks from botnet, the traditional network security architecture primarily chooses passive defense means. For example, most ISPs mainly utilize pattern matching [1], feature matching [2] and rule algorithms in DDoS attack detection [3], which reflect a slow response and high cost in tracing the attack [4]. Furthermore, as the high bandwidth, huge traffic and limited storage in ISPs' backbone, all the factors lead to a slow evolution in botnet detection and massive DDoS attacks rapidly intensified.

To deal with the rapidly intensified DDoS attack from cloud environment, a botnet situation awareness method was proposed which is based on big data analysis. By quickly and timely creating a botnet topology and DDoS attack traffic warning, it could effectively block the potential sources of large-scale DDoS attacks and improve the ISPs' active defense ability.

© Springer International Publishing Switzerland 2015
R. Cai et al. (Eds.): APWeb 2015 Workshops, LNCS 9461, pp. 71–78, 2015.
DOI: 10.1007/978-3-319-28121-6_7

2 Analysis of Botnet Situation Awareness Technology Based on Big Data in Cloud

Currently, to defense the botnet cloud, the most common way is just focusing on the top10 botnets based on the number of infected hosts, which cannot perceive the botnets' living state nor give the specific botnets in fast growing. Whereas in theory, the ability to perceive botnet situation is crucial to detect the botnets and resist DDoS attacks.

Many security systems like honeypots, the botnet detection clusters, the DDoS detection systems and traffic tracing systems, have been deployed in ISPs' networks. Although the systems could purify the Internet to some extent, some disadvantage cannot be ignored like different warning message formats in various systems, high redundancy in different systems' logs, simple but single function of each system and etc. All the deficiency result in the deployed defense architecture's inefficiency and ineffectiveness that useful warning could be flooded and separate security systems cannot interchange their own data and knowledge.

In order to overcome the shortcomings of the existing security system, a botnet situation awareness model is proposed based on a correlation analysis on different systems' logs, which could bring about effective warning and active defense of DDoS attack from botnet cloud.

Figure 1 is the diagrammatic pyramid sketch of the botnet situation awareness model. Firstly, a pre-process is made including events merging and correlation analysis on multi-source logs from different security systems like the honeypot, the botnet detection system, the DDoS detection system and the traffic tracing system. Secondly, a

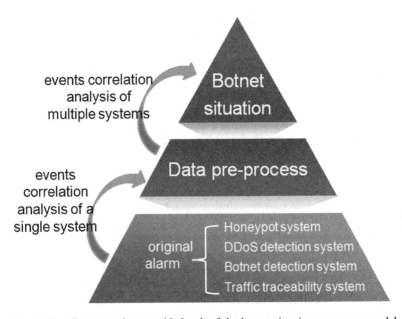

Fig. 1. The diagrammatic pyramid sketch of the botnet situation awareness model

deep correlation analysis is made on the preliminary results like the merged events by the big data aggregation and correlation analysis center. At last, a visualization of the botnet situation could be achieved, and the detection, tracking and alert of botnet would be made in cloud further.

3 Development and Deployment

3.1 Design of Botnet Situation Awareness Platform

Figure 2 exhibits the structure of the botnet situation awareness platform. The platform consolidates the honeypot, botnet detection system, DDoS detection system and traffic tracing system, integrates different functions including the events correlating, topology building, traffic alerting and etc. The elements for detection contain the control methods, propagation modes, range of influence, harm degree and etc (Table 1).

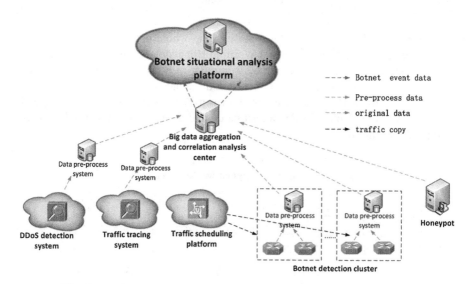

Fig. 2. Platform of botnet situation awareness based on big data in cloud

3.2 Pre-Process

In the process of an attack from a botnet cloud, different security system would separately produce a lot of raw warning data. It is ineffective to input the raw warning data directly into the botnet situation analysis platform as it is vast, redundant or even containing errors. Hence, the pre-process is essential. For single specific security equipment, it is important to make a simple correlation analysis on the original logs and merge the similar data to form a complete event.

An example of pre-process in Honeypot was given to show the limitation of traditional methods. Honeypot is used for trapping the Trojan Horse and detecting the

Table 1. Modules of Botnet Situation Awareness Platform

Module	Function
Botnet Situation Analysis Platform	Display the correlation result
Big data aggregation and correlation analysis center	Collect all the pre-processed data and make correlation analysis of different data from different devices
Data Pre-process System	Make pre-process of raw data including filtering, storage, merging and simple correlation analysis
DDoS detection system	Detect DDoS attack traffic incident
Traffic tracing system	Record the traffic information including the source/destination, IP/Port, and time stamp
Traffic scheduling platform	Copy and schedule the traffic in the Internet
Botnet detection cluster	Cluster of Deep-Packet-Inspection equipment to detect Botnet, Trojan Horse, Worm and computer virus
Honeypot	Detect the Suspicious attacks belonging to Intrusion Detection System

remote controller. By taking the Honeypot into the whole deployed IDS, IDS could detect the behavior of Trojan Horse and Worm in Honeypot, and further to achieve the IP address and Port number of the remote controller in botnet cloud. But the original warning data produced by IDS might be vast and redundant as it was triggered by an action of each Trojan Horse at once. As shown in Table 2, it is hard to show the IP address of the remote controller in Bonnet cloud and the range of influenced hosts by the original warning data.

Table 2. Example of original warning data in IDS

sourceIP address	Source port	Destination IP address	Destinatio n port	Trojan names	bulletCount
1.1.1.1	61373	2.2.2.2	5555	Trojan A	1
1.1.1.1	53464	3.3.3.3	5555	Trojan A	2

Compared to the traditional methods, our novel pre-process method was given including a correlation analysis and data merging of raw data from single equipment. It is easy to visualize the remote controller and the range of influenced hosts in botnet cloud no matter in the forward mode or the reverse mode.

1. As shown in Fig. 3, for a Trojan Horse warning generated by the IDS, if there is a source IP address mapping to a lot of different destination IP address but the same destination port, the Data Pre-process System would aggregate the similar warnings, form a botnet connecting event in the forward mode, and show the IP address of remote controller and the number of influenced hosts.

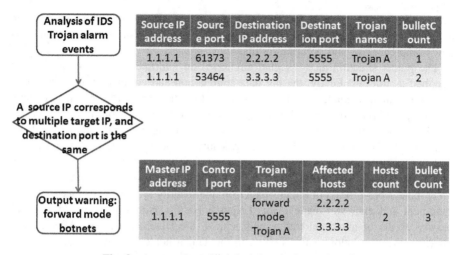

Fig. 3. Aggregation of original data in forward mode

2. As shown in Fig. 4, for a Trojan Horse warning generated by the IDS, if there is many different source IP addresses mapping to a single destination IP address and the same destination port, the Data Pre-process System would also aggregate the similar warnings, form a botnet connecting event in the reverse mode, and show the IP address of remote controller and the number of influenced hosts.

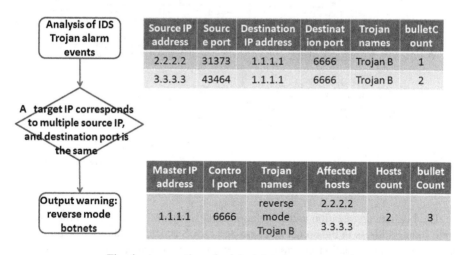

Fig. 4. Aggregation of original data in reverse mode

3.3 Analysis of Botnet Situation Awareness Based on Big Data

The botnet situation awareness platform mentioned in this paper consolidates different security systems including Honeypot, Botnet detection system, DDoS detection system and Traffic tracing system. It can make events merging, correlation analysis on multi-source logs, mine effective information about the botnet situation, and then draw more comprehensive and accurate results.

The botnet situation analysis platform based on multiple source logs analysis is described as follows. Firstly, the big data aggregation and correlation analysis center extracts essential attributes in the multi-source logs from multiple security systems. Secondly, it merges the original warning of the same IP address of attackers/victims. Thirdly, it evaluates the criticality of the aggregated warning and puts forward the accurate botnet alert which includes the criticality, range of infected hosts and the IP address of the remote controller in botnet cloud.

The process is displayed in Fig. 5, the big data aggregation and correlation analysis center make a pre-process of the raw data from the security systems like Honeypot, DPI equipment and etc., and achieve the Trajan horse list. Similarly, it could get DFI security events of abnormal traffic, and achieve the DDoS attack list. After that, it actualizes the correlation analysis between the Trajan horse list and the DDoS attack list. At last, the botnet situation analysis results can be concluded.

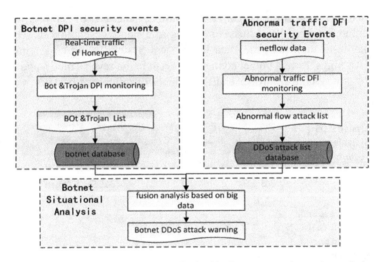

Fig. 5. Process of botnet situation awareness in the big data aggregation and correlation analysis center

The big data aggregation and correlation analysis center merges the warning of the same source address in the botnet database and DDoS attack list database, and then get the precise botnet situation information saved in the botnet situation analysis list (see Fig. 6). It can reduce the complexity of botnet analysis and make more precise results.

The big data aggregation and correlation analysis center analysis the botnet situation in two dimensions: the total number of the puppet machines and the increment speed of the puppet machines. This method can effectively catch sight of fast-growing botnet. So the fast-growing botnet could be cracked down in the early stage.

Botnet Database

Master IP address	port	Client IP address	Hosts count
1.1.1.1	5555	2.2.2.2	2
		3.3.3.3	

DDoS Attack List Database

Source IP addr	Destination IP addr	historical flow
2.2.2.2	9.9.9.9	200M bps
3.3.3.3	9.9.9.9	500M bps

fusion analysis based on big data

Botnet situation Analysis List

Master IP address	port	Client IP address	Hosts count	DDoS behavior	historical flow	Hazard level
1.1.1.1	5555	2.2.2.2	2	Yes	700M bps	middle
		3.3.3.3				

Fig. 6. Tables of botnet situation awareness in the big data aggregation and correlation analysis center

For example, the botnet with a remote controller using 1.1.1.1 IP address dominates n_1 puppet machines, and the peak attack traffic from the n_1 puppet machines was recorded as Q_1 Gbps. While in s days ago, the number of puppet machines was n_2. Based on the information above, some key indicators could be calculated as:

1. The increment speed of puppet machines dominated by the botnet:

$$v = \sqrt[s]{n_1/n_2} - 1$$

2. The number of remote controllers in t days later:

$$n = n_1(n_1/n_2)^{t/s}$$

3. The peak attack traffic from the botnet in t days later:

$$Q = Q_1(n_1/n_2)^{t/s}$$

To get a better observation of a botnet situation, the parameter t can also be set as hours, weeks and even months. It can effectively contribute to the active defense of DDoS attack by the botnet cloud.

4 Conclusions

The traditional methods to detect the botnet cloud are mainly based on the number of infected hosts, which lacks the awareness of botnet growing and cannot send the alerts of the fast-growing botnet cloud. This paper discusses the botnet situation awareness based on big data from multi-source logs. A botnet situation analysis platform was proposed with a pre-process of vast raw data and correlation analysis of events. By practice, it is superior to the traditional methods in detection accuracy and quick response of the botnet cloud.

Reference

1. Luo, Zhiqiang, Jun, Shen: Research and application of mobile e-commerce user provenance authentication technology. Telecommun. Sci. **6**, 7–12 (2009)
2. Jian, C., Fan, M.: Signatures extraction method based on classification of malicious software. J. Comput. Appl. **31**(1), 83–84 (2011)
3. Wang, Xinliang: Analysis and Detection of Botnet Anomaly Traffic[D]. Beijing University of Posts and Telecommunications, Beijing (2011)
4. Yu, Xiaocong, Dong, Xiaomei, Ge, Y., et al.: Online botnet detection techniques. Geomatics Inf. Sci. Wuhan Univ. **35**(15), 578–581 (2010)

Research on Cloud Datacenter Interconnect Technology

Nan Chen[✉], Yongbing Fan, Xiaowu He, Yi Liu, and Qiaoling Li

Guangdong Research Institute of China Telecom Co., Ltd.,
Guangzhou 510630, People's Republic of China
chenn@gsta.com

Abstract. The Cloud datacenter interconnect solution was proposed, specified in Cloud Management System (CMS), front-end network and back-end storage network. The characteristics of cloud application as well as the requirements of cloud datacenter interconnect were analyzed. The proposed solution satisfied the requirements of datacenter interconnect for cloud applications.

Keywords: IDC · DCI · Cloud computing

1 Introduction

More and more workloads are moving to cloud datacenters as a result of the largely adoption of cloud computing. The traffic in each area of the cloud datacenter is increasing dramatically since the application architecture is becoming cloud-aware, which means all the applications are carried by the unified cloud resource pool instead of the traditional monolithic multi-tier model. Enabling business continuity and speed of deployment are top concerns from the cloud service customer's perspective. It is required that the cloud datacenter network should be application-oriented [1] while the requirements of cloud datacenters interconnect (DCI) should also be analyzed and satisfied. The remain of this paper is organized as follows: Sect. 2 analyses the characteristics of cloud application as well as the requirements for DCI, while Sect. 3 proposed cloud datacenter interconnect solution. The conclusion and the further work have been introduced in Sect. 4.

2 Characteristics and DCI Requirements of Cloud Application

2.1 Characteristics of Cloud Application

The cloud application is decoupled from the underlying resource, so that the deployment is more flexible. The application consumes resources on some specified area within a cloud DC or even across the cloud DC infrastructure. The application is mobility using the VM live migration technology, which means that the application can be migrated across different locations without interruption. In that case, it is required that the DCI extends the application environment across multiple sites. The architecture

© Springer International Publishing Switzerland 2015
R. Cai et al. (Eds.): APWeb 2015 Workshops, LNCS 9461, pp. 79–86, 2015.
DOI: 10.1007/978-3-319-28121-6_8

of cloud application is flexible with scale-out/in capability to satisfy the rapid change of customer's demand dynamically. The cloud application is multi-tenancy while the tenant-based service can be provided to CSC. Last but not least, the cloud application is high service-continuity that the disaster and recovery of cloud application can be implemented under limited RPO/RTO when the underlay resource is interrupt or failures.

2.2 Requirements of Date Center Interconnect

In general, three different types of interconnection should be considered as follows:

1. Cloud Management System (CMS): The Cloud Management System (CMS) combines software and technologies in a design for managing cloud environments including manage a pool of heterogeneous compute-resources, provide access to end users, monitor security, manage resource allocation and manage tracking. Mostly, the administration domain is limited within datacenter, the CMS interconnect including information/database flow for multi-site synchronization.
2. Front-end Network: Different from the back-end storage network, the front-end network should satisfy the variety of cloud application requirements for DCI scenario, such as L2 extension, flexible VPC (tenant-based L2/L3 segment), tenant-based network QoS(bandwidth, latency, jitter), etc. DCI path optimization should also be considered to avoid traffic circle when the application has been migrated. Particularly, VM migration should be considered very carefully. Different virtualization software comes with different network requirements. In general, the restriction factors, including L2 network connectivity, RTT and bandwidth[1,] is reducing.
3. Back-end Storage Network: The SAN/NAS have been wildly deployed in cloud DC along with server virtualization technology. The storage network among different sites should be synchronous or quasi-synchronous to satisfy the requirements of inter-datacenter deployment, workload mobility, and disaster recovery. In fact, the storage consistent is the most critical constraints for DCI.

The network requirements for DCI are proposed as follow:

1. LAN (L2) Extension: L2 connectivity among different sites for front-end network to satisfy the requirements of VM migration, across sites application environment, disaster recovery and VPC. The IP and MAC address of migrated VM should not be changed, as well as the status of L4 ~ 7 stateful services should also be maintained.
2. Path Optimize: The traffic from remote cline to migrated VM, which located in another datacenter, should be avoided to go through the original datacenter. The traffic to remote cline from migrated VM should also be steered to the new gateway instead of the original one. However, the gateway configuration for the migrated VM does not change automatically.

---

[1] VMware vSphere 6.0: Support L3 network, 100 ms RTT.

3. Failures Isolation: The broadcast storm only affects the L2 domain within date center, the remote datacenter should not be influenced even if a L2 extension environment is provided across datacenters. The failures/interruption of particular link or equipment should also be isolated within the datacenter and should not be dispersed to other datacenters through L2 DCI connectivity.

4. Storage Consistent: The back-end storage network should be synchronous/quasi-synchronous in order to satisfy the requirements such as VM live migration, database cluster, disaster and recovery.

3   Cloud Datacenter DCI Solution

The cloud datacenter DCI solution is illustrated as Fig. 1. Interconnection on each layers, including CMS, front-end network and back-end network have been introduced respectively based on the application-oriented cloud datacenter network architecture [1].

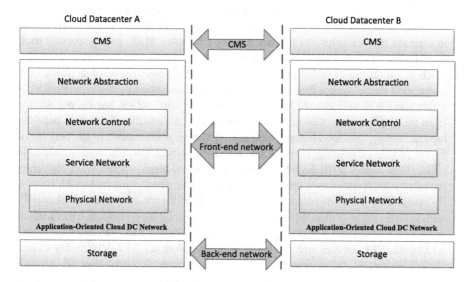

Fig. 1. Cloud datacenter DCI

3.1   Cloud Management System (CMS)

Each datacenter has its own Cloud Management System (CMS) with independent administration domain, so that each CMS can manage the single cloud datacenter site and isolate the failure. CMS leverages network orchestration capability by northbound interface of SDN controller to provision and manage the whole network within datacenter. The CMS cascading solution [3] or unified portal can be used for multi datacenters interconnect. The unified portal provides single point access to Cloud Service Customer with resource/service management and OAM for all cloud datacenters.

3.2   Front-End Network

The front-end network which carried service and migration traffic is required to leverage LAN extension technology to provide L2 connectivity across different sites. The control plane, data plane as well as the deploy model have been introduced as follow.

LAN (L2) Extension. The LAN extension technology, which can be classified in 3 different types based on the interconnect layer, and the possible scenario have been analyzed as follow:

1. Physical-Link-based: The datacenters are directly connected by physical link leveraging dark fiber, DWDM or OTN. It is suitable for limited scale of sites, no-faraway distance and simple topology.
2. MPLS-based: The gateway (PE) establishes L2 VPN based on MPLS leveraging VLL, VPLS, PBB-VPLS, EVPN or PBB-EVPN. VLL provides P2P logical L2 link, while VPLS provides P2MP logical links. The network configuration of both technologies are complex, meanwhile both technologies have the problem of limitation of MAC address table size, low performance of network converge, inflexible VPN topology and policy. PBB-VPLS combines the PBB and VPLS technologies to increase the scalability of the network by providing MAC hiding, service multiplexing and pseudowire aggregation while still have the same problem as VPLS (such as limitation of MAC address table size, low performance of network converge, etc.) as the control protocol still using data-plane flooding mechanism. EVPN using control-plane based MAC learning over the core, which has been designed from the ground up to handle sophisticated access redundancy scenarios, per-flow load balancing, and operational simplicity. PBB-EVPN inherits all of the benefits of EVPN, while combining PBB (IEEE 802.1ah) and EVPN functions in a single node. This allows PBB-EVPN to simplify control-plane operation in the core, provide faster convergence and enhance scalability, when compared to EVPN.
3. IP-based: The datacenters are connected by IP network leveraging VLLoGRE/VPLSoGRE, OTV, VxLAN/NVGRE. The topology, L2 loop avoidance mechanism of VLLoGRE/VPLSoGRE is very similar to MPLS-based VLL/VPLS which means VLLoGRE/VPLSoGRE still have the same problem as VLL/VPLS. OTV is a "MAC address in IP" technique for supporting Layer 2 VPNs over IP network while using a control protocol to advertise MAC address reachability information (instead of using data plane learning) and packet switching of IP encapsulated Layer 2 traffic (instead of using circuit switching) for data forwarding. OTV usually uses the IP multicast capabilities of the core[2], and the scale of DCI is limited to 4 site[3]. VxLAN uses a VLAN-like encapsulation technique to encapsulate MAC-based OSI layer 2 Ethernet frames within layer 4 UDP packets, while increasing scalability up to 16 million logical networks and allows for layer 2 adjacency across IP networks. NVGRE uses a Generic Routing Encapsulation (GRE) to create an isolated virtual

---

[2] However, it can use IP unicast capabilities of the core, but the performance is not as well as using IP multicast capabilities.

[3] Each site has 2 nodes maximum.

Layer 2 network that may be confined to a single physical Layer 2 network or extend across subnet boundaries while identifying a 24-bit Tenant Network Identifier (TNI) to address multi-tenant network. There are 3 different types of control plane solution: data-flow driven (IP multicast), NEV control plane driven (BGP) and NVE data plane driven (SDN controller). VxLAN/NVGRE-based solutions are the major solution for the intra-datacenter scenario, however, multi-homing, failures isolation, are still the open issue for DCI scenario when using VxLAN/NVGRE directly across multi sites.

Physical-Link-based DCI solution should be used for regional datacenter DCI scenario, while the VPLS and physical-link-based solution should be used for small-scale DCI scenario. The EVPN and PBB-EVPN solutions should be used for large-scale DCI scenario while the standardization is not mature enough. However, EVPN/PBB-EVPN is recommended for this solution.

Deploy Model. The VxLAN Gateway and the WAN Edge (PE) functions can be decoupled in two separate systems or integrated into the same system. The former option will be referred as "Decoupled Interconnect solution" whereas the latter one will be referred as "Integrated Interconnect solution". Figure 2 shows both deploy models. For Decoupled Interconnect solution, the MAC-VRF instance on gateways should provide interconnect to heterogeneous WAN networks while the gateway can use VNIDs as local or global values. The overlay network within datacenter can be protected and isolated under this solution. The QoS/ACL enforcement and OAM is clear and simple demarcation for Decoupled Interconnect solution and the control plane interactions between DC gateways and WAN PEs is minimum. When the DC and the WAN are operated by the same administrative entity, the Service Provider can decide to integrate the gateway and WAN edge PE functions in the same router for obvious CAPEX and OPEX saving reasons, which refers to "Integrated Interconnect solution".

Control Plane. The control plane of core should be separated among intra datacenter networks, while the SDN controller is usually used as control plane within datacenter to provide unified network resource, topology, routing management and service provision. The datacenter gateway should allocates a VNID per a VPN label when getting route from PE, also it should allocate an MPLS label per < NVE and VNID > when getting route from an NVE. The control plane between datacenters should be used BGP MAC/B-MAC Advertisement Route for EVPN/PBB-EVPN, which will be used in data plane. The multicast route to distribute the VNI information over the MPLS network should include the discovery of the PEs participating in a given VNI and Stitching of the IP multicast trees, local to each VXLAN site with the LSM trees of the MPLS network. The MAC mobility only propagated for mac-moves between DCs.

Path Optimize. The path optimizes solutions with two different scenarios should be used as follow:

1. Traffic from remote cline to VM: The remote cline always queries a DNS server to resolve VM IP address. The DNS server replies new IP address for the migrated VM located in another DC to remote cline when the VM has been migrated. The DNS server and network control has been tightly coupled in such situation.

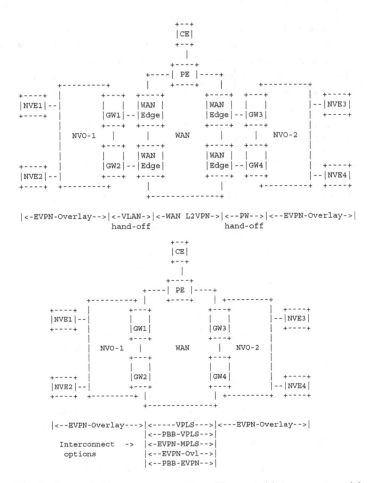

Fig. 2. Decoupled interconnect model and integrated interconnect model

2. Traffic from VM to remote cline: It is possible to deploy a local active default gateway for all the hosts belonging to a given extended VLAN. The same virtual MAC (vMAC) and virtual IP (vIP) are associated to the default gateway active in each location. A VM migrated between DC1 and DC2 would maintain in the ARP cache the information it had before moving, so the same (vMAC, vIP) combination can be used to route traffic outside its own subnet once migrated to the new location.

Failures Isolation. The STP isolation, flood storms suppression, split horizon have been used for DCI failures isolation.

1. STP Isolation: The BPDU feature on the gateway has been disabling for DCI population in order to isolate the spanning tree domains between the data centers.
2. Flood Storms Suppression: The unknown unicast and broadcast frames should be suppress to populate across datacenters by using ARP proxy or BGP.

3. Split Horizon: The PE should de-encapsulate the frames from core and only forward inside the datacenter in order to prevent loop between sites.

Data Plane. The VM MAC address will be learned in data plane from the VxLAN network while the VM address will be learnt over MPLS/IP core in control plane for EVPN (in data plane for PBB-EVPN). L2 unicast traffic destined to the VxLAN network will be encapsulated with the IP/UDP header + customer bridge VNI while L2 unicast traffic destined to the MPLS/IP network will be encapsulated with the MPLS label. Each VxLAN network independently builds its P2MP or MP2MP shared multicast trees for one or more VNIs. In the MPLS/IP network, multiple options are available for the delivery of multicast traffic, such as ingress replication and LSM options. There is no packet duplication, forwarding loops and multicast stitching with per-VNI load balancing for Multi-homing VxlAN network. The datacenter gateway should maintain incoming and outgoing forwarding table and stitching VxLAN tunnel and MPLS VPN tunnel with no payload lookup. The incoming forwarding table is an entry has the mapping of MPLS label to < NVE ip address, VNID > while the outgoing forwarding table is an entry has the mapping of VNID to MPLS label. The stitching must ensure for Multi-homing VXLAN network with no packet duplication, no forwarding loops and the multicast stitching should be with per VNI load balancing. There is no change in the EVPN procedures for split-horizon at the NVEs.

3.3   Back-End Storage Network

It is critical to ensure the VM which may migrate between datacenters access to the storage consistently. There are two different types of storage technology could be used as follow:

1. Shared storage: all the VM access to the same physical storage that is deployed in a specific data center location, the storage extension technology is leveraged to provide access to VM when the it migrated to other datacenters. The distance between datacenters is limited as the IO delay and performance is not acceptable for a long-distance scenario.
2. Active/active storage: The VM can access to the local storage that is deployed in each datacenter. The backend storage network will synchronous the data in separate sites. Also, the constraints for storage network data synchronous are critical.

4   Conclusion and Future Work

The solution of Cloud Management System, front-end network carried service, management and migration traffic and the front-end storage network interconnect has been introduced in this paper which should be satisfied the requirements of cloud application analyzed in Sect. 2. However, only technology analysis and the solution have been proposed without any experimental or production network deployment results. The next step should focus on the verification and deployment in LAB and also in production environment.

References

1. Hong, T., Nan, C.: Analysis on cloud datacenter evolution. Telecommun. Sci. **10**(6), 30–35 (2011)
2. Chen, N., Fan, Y., He, X., Liu, Y., Huang, Z.: Research on application-oriented cloud data center network technology. Telecommun. Sci. **9**, 128–132 (2014)
3. OpenStack cascading solution. https://wiki.openstack.org/wiki/OpenStack_cascading_solution
4. IETF RFC 7432, BGP MPLS-Based Ethernet VPN
5. IETF draft, BESS Workgroup, Interconnect Solution for EVPN Overlay networks
6. IETF RFC 7365, Framework for Datacenter (DC) Network Virtualization

Summarization-Based Ensemble Learning Method for Sparsely Labeled Webpage Classification

Le Li[1,2]([✉]), Junyi Xu[1], Haiming Tong[2], and Weidong Xiao[1]

[1] College of Information System and Management,
National University of Defense Technology, Changsha, China
lile10@126.com
[2] China Satellite Maritime Tracking and Control Department, Jiangyin, China

Abstract. Sparsely labeled problem has been arisen in webpage classification field recently. In this paper, we propose a summarization-based ensemble learning method for handling this problem. Directory compression strategy is used to reduce the scale of webpages to be crawled, so existing knowledge can accumulate to guide subsequent classification process. Then, smart summarization strategy is applied to get concise content of webpages, which overcomes the impact of noise and obtains more related text features. Experiments on public dataset reveal that the proposed method can obtain competing classification result when the dataset is labeled sparsely.

Keywords: Sparsely labeled classification · Summarization · Webpage classification

1 Introduction

Due to the wide application on question answering systems [1,2], recommendations [3] and information retrieval [4,5], webpage classification is still one of the most important challenges in big data era. Traditional classification methods often rely on content of the webpages, where the text in different position (title, body) tends to have a different weight. However, the webpages are semistructured documents in HTML format [6], which are diverse and complex, it is difficult to extract text and related information accurately; In addition, there are a lot of advertisement on the webpages, which will bring many noisy data to the classification task. Extracting latent features is a kind of effective strategies. For example, we can obtain the latent topics [7] in each webpage firstly, and make prediction according to the similarity on topics. However, the performance of these methods is greatly affected by parameters, and extracting topic often requires a certain computing time, making it difficult to deal with real-time classification scenes.

While the rapid development of information technology has greatly improved our ability to collect data in recent years, traditional classification methods are

© Springer International Publishing Switzerland 2015
R. Cai et al. (Eds.): APWeb 2015 Workshops, LNCS 9461, pp. 87–97, 2015.
DOI: 10.1007/978-3-319-28121-6_9

facing new challenges. Due to limited capacity of manual tagging, labeled data increase much slowly. In most cases, we need to use lower labeled proportion data to make prediction. This makes the sparsely labeled classification [8,9] problem particularly evident in the big data era. For example, in the traditional classification task, we often use 90 % labeled data to predict 10 % unknown data, but now we only have 10 % or even 1 % of the labeled data. So we need to extract more effective features, which can overcome the noise data, and make prediction fast and accurately.

In this paper, we present a summarization-based ensemble learning method to deal with the sparsely labeled challenges in webpage classification. By introducing the directory compression strategy, our approach can reduce the number of pages to be classified greatly, and improve the speed of classification effectively; In addition, we propose a smart-summarization method by using search engine, which can overcome impact of noisy data and extract text features accurately. Meanwhile, this summarization strategy can greatly reduce the vocabulary space, making the complexity of classification model greatly reduced. Experimental results show that our method performs competitively on real world datasets, and can overcome the sparsely labeled challenge effectively.

2   Related Works

Directly using the content in the webpage will be affected by many noisy data, so latent features methods are proposed to get high-level content. An article may discuss the contents of multiple topics, such as travel, picture and reading. Therefore, the latent topic can be used to build the text feature of documents. The noisy data can be extracted as independent topics, which may be different in each article, but the similar articles will share more similar topics. LDA [7] is a widely used topic model, which can model documents to word-topic distribution and topic-document distribution. Author Topic model [10] is a probabilistic topic model to study the relationship between author and text, but in the webpage, it does not contain authors information usually. These methods need certain time to extract topic and the performance is greatly affected by parameters. To handle the sparsely labeled classification task, we aim to design more efficient method without many parameters.

Webpages classification is different from text classification [6]. The webpages are semi-structured documents in HTML, so it is not easy to extract the related content accurately. In big data era, the layout of webpages is diverse, so there is no universal method to get the main part of the webpages. Therefore, directly crawling the webpage will obtain many noisy data. In addition, webpages contain a unique feature: URL, which can be used to make prediction independently. For example, [11] demonstrated that URL-based method is magnitudes faster than typical web page classification, as the pages themselves do not have to be fetched and analyzed. In addition, [12] pointed that when treated correctly, URL-based exceeds the performance of some source-document based features. [13] applied a machine learning approach to the topic identification task, and reveal that all-grams as features can gave the best results and Tokens as features the worst.

3 Framework for Summarization-Based Ensemble Learning

3.1 Intuition

The most common problem in webpage classification is that, only given URL of the webpages, how to predict the label of the webpage accurately.

In some cases, URL contains keywords in related areas (hotel, pic, etc.), so these keywords can be uses to predict category of the URL. For example, we can extract the keyword sport in the URL: http://sports.sina.com.cn/j/2015-04-20/ 21287581972.shtml, which indicted that this webpage is related to the *sport* category. However, further analysis found that only using keywords in URL will encounter two challenges:

(1) No keywords in URL. For example, we cannot find any keyword in the URL: http://hs.tgbus.com/db/a/1048.shtml, but actually this webpage belongs to a very famous games website. Therefore, only using keywords in URL cannot classify this kind of webpages.
(2) Too many keywords in URL. We focus on single-label classification task in this paper, which means a URL is only related with on label. But in some URLs, they contain multiple keywords, for example, there are two keywords *hotel* and *pic* in http://sports.163.com/photo/. In this case, only using keywords in URL is hard to distinguish which is the better choice of these two labels.

Therefore, only using the keywords in URL is not enough to make accurate prediction. We need to extend the feature space, and include more related information to improve the classification performance.

In addition to URL, the most obvious feature is content in webpages. We can open the URL in the explorer, crawl and parse the content, which is shown in Fig.1.

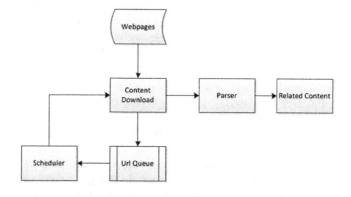

Fig. 1. Crawl the webpage

However, two problems arise when directly using the text in each webpage. Firstly, in big data era, there will be a very large amount of webpages need to be predicted. It will take a lot of time to crawl each webpage and analyze the text. Secondly, contents in the webpage are usually much longer, complex and noisy. Unrelated recommendations and advertisements will bring many noisy data for text analysis process.

We design a summarization-based ensemble learning method to handle all the above problems. Directory compression strategy is used to reduce the scale of webpages to be classified. The existing knowledge can be reused for prediction, which improves the classification speed; smart summarization strategy is applied to get the concise description about the webpage, which can overcome the noisy data effectively; the results of URL-keywords-based classifier and text classifier are combined by voting, which has more powerful generalization ability than a single classifier. The framework of our method is shown in Fig.2.

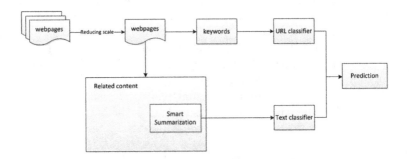

Fig. 2. Framework of summarization-based ensemble learning method

3.2 Directory Compression

When there are a large amount of pages need to be predicted, directly analyzing each webpage will consume a lot of time. We aim to design a more efficient method, which does not need to crawl and analyze each webpage. The intuition is to make cluster of these webpages. However, traditional method like K-means still needs to crawl every webpage. We try to handle this problem from another perspective. For most websites, the architecture is clear. Related contents are well organized and posted on the specific subdirectory. For example, the webpage (http://sports.sina.com.cn/china/j/2015-09-15/doc-ifxhupik6862196.shtml) discussed news in Chinese Football Association Super League (CSL), will be posted on the specific directory: http://sports.sina.com.cn/china/. And all the related content about CSL will be posted on http://sports.sina.com.cn/. Therefore, we can find that the label of webpage is closely related with the upper directory. So we do not need to crawl and parse the contents of every webpage, using the related content in up-directory can be a more effective way to predict the current webpage category. The use of such a compression strategy is very effective, for example, given the dataset in experiment section, the number of pages need to be crawled can be compressed as follows (Fig. 3):

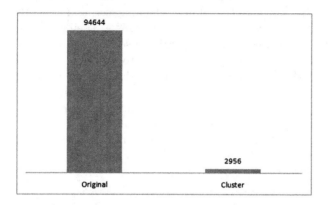

Fig. 3. Compression performance

3.3 Smart Summarization

By introducing directory compression strategy, there are less pages need to be crawled. However, the contents in upper directory webpage are still too long, and contain many noisy data. Although the scale of the text can be reduced by making text summarization [14], it is difficult to obtain high quality content. We try to solve this problem in a different perspective.

One of the biggest changes the 21th century was that we can obtain accurate result through Google, Baidu and other search engines efficiently. Recalling the searching process we will find that given some keywords, search engines will present to us a summary content, rather than all the relevant content. It means that in the information retrieval process, search engine has already made smart summarization, and the related contents are compressed from pages to one or two sentences. This short summarization is of great value, which has filtered out a lot of useless noise data, and reflects the most relevant content. Therefore, instead of using specific text summarization method, we apply the search engines to get the concise description.

3.4 Ensemble Learning

Existing researches have shown that the ensemble method has more powerful generalization ability than a single classifier. Now we have the information of URLs and the related text description, so we construct the URL classifier and text classifier respectively, and make prediction by voting.

4   Detailed Design

4.1   Framework of Training and Testing Processes

For the training set, we aim to extract the label-related text. For example, we collect all the URLs of **sport** label in the training set, and crawl through search engines to extract the summarization of these URLs. Then we will get the "label-summarization" knowledge K1 in the training set.

For the test set, the primary purpose is to find the associated text for a given URL. Firstly, we will check K1 to find the relevant information. If there are related contents in K1, the URL can be classified by using the contents directly. Otherwise, we still need to use search engines to find text feature for classification, and update the knowledge base K1.

The training and testing processes are shown in Figs. 4 and 5 respectively.

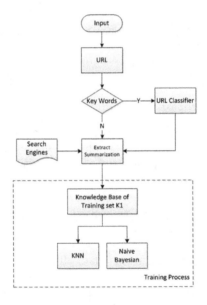

Fig. 4. Training process

4.2   URL Classifier

The core idea for the URL classifier is to extract and estimate the keywords. The weight of each word is different, greater weight obtained when it is more close to the domain. For example, given the URL:http://comment.sports.163. com/cache/newlist/sports_bbs/AM2LMAPN00051C8M_1.html

We can extract the keywords: *sport* and *comment*, but the weights of each word are different, which are set 2 and 1 respectively.

For the training set, we can construct a label-keywords matrix, and an element $F(A, B)$ in the matrix means given a URL contains keyword B, the URL

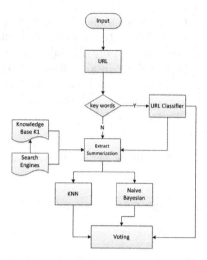

Fig. 5. Testing process

has $F(a, b)$ probability that belong to category A. Therefore, the prediction process for URL classifier is as follows:

Given an URL: U,

1. Extracting key words in U: $k_1, \ldots, k_n$
2. The weight of each word can be calculated: $w_1, \ldots, w_n$
3. The score of U belong to C_j is: $S(C_j) = \prod\limits_{i=1}^{n} w_i \cdot F(C_j, k_i)$

4.3 Text Classifier

After extracting the summarization, text classifier will be used to make prediction from the perspective of text feature. Several preprocessing steps are applied for the related content, such as making words segmentation, filtering noisy data and removing lower frequency words. And then, TFIDF (term frequency Cinverse document frequency) technique is used to measure the importance of words.

KNN (K-Nearest Neighbor) and Naive Bayesian method are most famous machine learning models for handling the text classification task. Therefore, we applied both of them to make prediction independently. In KNN model, cosine similarity is used to measure distance between cases.

5 Experiment

5.1 Dataset

We evaluate the proposed method for the performance of classification on the following real-world dataset. In The 17th Asia Pacific Web Conference

(APWeb2015), China Telecom held a data challenge [15], which provided 10,000,000 URLs but only 100,000 of them with label information. The challenge required the participants to use only 1% labeled data to predict the rest part. We used the training set, which contains about 100,000 URLs and labeled information, to evaluate the proposed method. In the dataset, each line represents a training case, which contains two columns, URL and the label, and the two columns are separated by tab, which is shown in Table 1.

Table 1. Training case in the dataset

URL	Classification
http://sports.sina.com.cn/j/2015-04-20/21287581972.shtml	9001004000000

The descriptions of the labels are as shown in Table 2.

Table 2. Descriptions of dataset label

Label	Descriptions
9001004000000	Information-Sport
9001006000000	Information-Travel
9001007000000	Information-Finance
9001013000000	Information-Health
9002001000000	Entertainment-Music
9002002000000	Entertainment-Video
9002003000000	Entertainment-Reading
9002004000000	Entertainment-Cartoon
9002005000000	Entertainment-Picture
9002006000000	Entertainment-Game

Each URL is related with one label. Data set contains a total of 10 labels, which are *Sport*, *Travel*, *Finance*, *Health*, *Music*, *Video*, *Reading*, *Cartoon*, *Picture* and *Game*.

5.2 Classification Results

In the experiment, we use accuracy as an evaluation measurement to evaluate the classification performance. In each experiment, we divide the dataset into two sets of training data and test data, while cases in the training data are labeled, cases in the test data are set unknown. Labeled cases in the training data are then used to predict labels of the test data. We focus on the classification performance on sparsely labeled proportion. Therefore, we vary the labeled proportion (lower than 10 %) and evaluate the performance of different methods.

Firstly, we only use the text feature, and compare the performance of several single classifiers: KNN, NB (Naive Bayesian) and SGD (Stochastic gradient descent). The performances of different methods are plotted in Fig. 6.

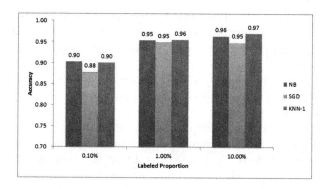

Fig. 6. Performances of single classifiers

We can find that when the labeled proportion decreased from 10 % to 0.1 %, the accuracy of all the three methods also decreased from 0.96 to 0.9, which means that sparsely labeled problem did affect the performance of classifiers. And as can be seen, the performances of Naive Bayesian and KNN are more satisfied, so we choose both of them as base classifiers in the following ensemble learning process.

Now, we integrated the result of URL classifier and text classifier to make prediction by voting. We varied the labeled proportion (lower than 10 %) and the performance of the ensemble learning method is plotted in Fig. 7. As can be

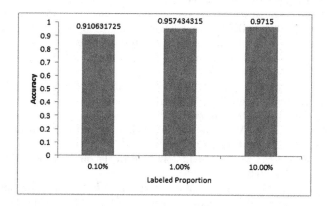

Fig. 7. Performances of ensemble learning method

seen, the performances of ensemble learning method have been improved on all the three labeled proportion, which has shown that our method can overcome the sparsely labeled problem effectively.

6 Conclusion

We design an efficient method to handle the sparsely labeled classification task in big data era. By introducing upper directory strategy, we compressed the scale of webpages greatly. And by using the search engine-based summarization method, we can get more concise text. Then URL classifier and text classifiers are combined to make prediction, which improve the generalization ability than a single classifier. Experiment result shows that our method can handle the sparsely labeled task effectively.

Due to the limited time and computing constraint, the model can be improved from several perspectives. For example, we can introduce multi-source information fusion strategy. This is because we found that the focus of different search engine is different, making the related data obtained are also differ. We cannot judge which search engine has a better performance, so randomly using single information source may lead to large errors. Therefore, we can combine more search engines results together, and screen more implied knowledge to get better performance.

References

1. Yang, H., Chua, T.S.: Effectiveness of web page classification on finding list answers. In: Proceedings of the 27th Annual International ACM SIGIR Conference on Research and Development in Information Retrieval, pp. 522–523. ACM (2004)
2. Yang, H., Chua, T.S.: Web-based list question answering. In: Proceedings of the 20th International Conference on Computational Linguistics, p. 1277. Association for Computational Linguistics(2004)
3. Nguyen, T.T.S., Lu, H.Y., Lu, J.: Web-page recommendation based on web usage and domain knowledge. IEEE Trans. Knowl. Data Eng. 26(10), 2574–2587 (2014)
4. Käki, M.: Findex: search result categories help users when document ranking fails. In: Proceedings of the SIGCHI Conference on Human Factors in Computing Systems, pp. 131–140. ACM (2005)
5. Kohlschütter, C., Chirita, P.A., Nejdl, W.: Utility analysis for topically biased pagerank. In: Proceedings of the 16th International Conference on World Wide Web, pp. 1211–1212. ACM (2007)
6. Qi, X., Davison, B.D.: Web page classification: features and algorithms. ACM Comput. Surv. (CSUR) 41(2), 12 (2009)
7. Blei, D.M., Ng, A.Y., Jordan, M.I.: Latent dirichlet allocation. J. Mach. Learn. Res. 3, 993–1022 (2003)
8. Widyantoro, D.H., Yen, J.: Relevant data expansion for learning concept drift from sparsely labeled data. IEEE Trans. Knowl. Data Eng. 17(3), 401–412 (2005)

9. Gallagher, B., Tong, H., Eliassi-Rad, T., Faloutsos, C.: Using ghost edges for classification in sparsely labeled networks. In: Proceedings of the 14th ACM SIGKDD International Conference on Knowledge Discovery and Data Mining, pp. 256–264. ACM (2008)

10. Steyvers, M., Smyth, P., Rosen-Zvi, M., Griffiths, T.: Probabilistic author-topic models for information discovery. In: Proceedings of the Tenth ACM SIGKDD International Conference on Knowledge Discovery and Data Mining, pp. 306–315. ACM (2004)

11. Kan, M.Y.: Web page categorization without the web page. In: World Wide Web Conference Series (2004)

12. Kan, M.Y., Thi, H.O.N.: Fast webpage classification using url features. In: The 14th ACM International Conference on Information and Knowledge Management (CIKM), pp. 325–326 (2005)

13. Baykan, E., Henzinger, M., Marian, L., Weber, I.: Purely url-based topic classification. In: Proceedings of International Conference on World Wide Web 3(10), pp. 1689–1694 (2009)

14. Shen, D., Chen, Z., Yang, Q., Zeng, H.J., Zhang, B., Lu, Y., Ma, W.Y.: Webpage classification through summarization. In: Proceedings of Sheffield SIGIR - Twenty-Seventh Annual International ACM SIGIR Conference on Research and Development in Information Retrieval (2004)

15. http://www.dmirlab.com/apweb2015/data-challenge.html

BSD

Collaborative Model for Predicting Retweeting Behaviors on Twitter

Liang Guo[✉], Zhaoyun Ding, Sheng Zhang, Taowei Li,
Weiwei Jiang, and Hui Wang

College of Information Systems and Management,
National University of Defense Technology,
Changsha 410073, Hunan, People's Republic of China
{guoliang,zyding,zhangsheng,litaowei,jiangweiwei,huiwang}@nudt.edu.cn

Abstract. Nowadays, Twitter has become one of the most important ways for information sharing. Users can spread information they like by retweeting. However, with the growth of twitter, users are easily overwhelmed by large amount of data and it is very diffcult for users to dig out information that they are interested in. To address this problem, we predict tweets that users are really interested in and help them reduce the effort to find useful information. In this paper, we introduce the users' similarity and trust based on retweeting behaviors and propose a retweeting behaviors prediction model based on collaborative filtering. The experiments show that our model was applicable on the real-life data.

Keywords: Retweeting behaviors · Predict model · Collaborative filtering · Twitter

1 Introduction

Recently, twitter has become a popular microblogging platform that enables users to share information by sending short 140-character messages. Until now, it has nearly 302 million users, who generates 500 million tweets per day. Users can get timeline of specific persons' tweets by following them. However, with the rapidly increasing number of tweets, users especially those follow many persons' are facing a serious problem of information overload. The useful tweets for the user may be flooded by other tweets that the user does not care about at all. So predicting the tweets that user cared so much is a huge challenge [1]. Then what kind of tweets a user cared so much? Intuitively, it is determined by many factors, such as the users' personal interest, the retweeting times, the content of the tweet, etc. Among these factors, the personal interest is the most important. Unlike existing work, which always analyzes the content of tweets and uses social relationship, we introduced the similarity and the trust between the users based on the retweeting behaviors.

Twitter has a retweet mechanism that is to repost a message from another twitter user and share it with one's own followers. It can accelerate the spread

© Springer International Publishing Switzerland 2015
R. Cai et al. (Eds.): APWeb 2015 Workshops, LNCS 9461, pp. 101–112, 2015.
DOI: 10.1007/978-3-319-28121-6_10

of information and show the users' personal interests [2]. As tweets are used many different languages and users' personal interests may change with times, traditional methods like analyzing the content are difficult to discover the users' interests [3]. So we proposed a predicting retweeting behaviors model based on collaborative filtering. As the Fig. 1 shown, our model is based on data collection and preprocessing; and its main components,including (1) Computing user-tweet interest based on trust, (2) Computing user-tweet interest based on similarity, (3) Computing user-tweet interest based on weighted interest.

Data collection and preprocessing: To address the problem, we used Twitter API to crawl tweets and users' information based on several randomly selected

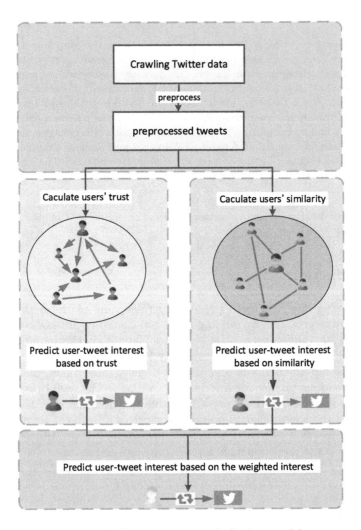

Fig. 1. Predicting retweeting behaviors model

users and expand users by accessing their followers and followees links. In the preprocessing, we extracted retweeted users' screennames by matching *RT@* and cut off the first 30 characters from the tweet text which removed retweeted users' screennames and mentioned users' screennames as the tag of the tweet.

Computing user-tweet interest based on trust: Intuitively, if a user always retweet tweets which the user v post, there is a strong possibility that the user will retweet the tweet which the user v post in the future. So we introduce the trust feature to predict the strength of the user's interest in a tweet.

Computing user-tweet interest based on similarity: Based on traditional collaborative filtering, we computed the similarity between users according to the retweeted relation and predicted the strength of the user's interest in a tweet.

Computing user-tweet interest based on weighted interest: After previous two steps, we propose a weighted formula to compute the user-tweet interest by integrating the strength of the user's interest based on trust and similarity.

Here, we make two assumption:

(1) If a user retweet a tweet, the user should be similar with users who also retweeted the tweet and be trust to the user who post the tweet.
(2) Users are likely to retweet the tweet which is retweeted by similar users or post by trustworthy users.

These assumptions make our model applicable to predict tweets. The remainder of this paper is organized as follows. Related work is discussed in Sect. 2. In Sect. 3, we describe the collaborative model for predicting retweeting behaviors. In Sect. 4, we present the results of our experiments and evaluate the effectiveness of our methodology compared with other baseline methods. Finally, conclusion and future works are given in Sect. 5.

2   Related Work

Collaborative filtering aims to do recommendation by finding users with similar preferences or items with similar properties based on a large number of users' ratings. In contrast to content-based Filtering, it doesn't consider content and totally based on user interactive information and historical items. In many scenarios, especially the lack of information about users' and items' description, collaborative filtering has great advantages. Nowadays, collective filtering has implemented in many large commercial systems, such as news recommendation in GroupLens movies, movies recommendation in MovieLens and music recommendation in Ringo , etc. Collaborative Filtering can be divided into two categories, neighborhood-based methods [4] and model-based methods [5].

Neighborhood-based methods have two basic assumptions below:

1. Users who rated similar in the past are likely to rate similar to the new item.
2. Items which got similar ratings in the past are likely to get similar ratings from the new user.

There have two methods called user-based collaborative filtering based on the first assumption and item-based collaborative filtering based on the second assumption respectively. Both methods essentially filter out irrelevant ratings information and do recommendation according to most similar user-item ratings information. Therefore, calculating similarity is important in neighborhood-based methods. Many works integrate a lot of features to calculate the similarity between users or items. Such as behaviors' time series, social relationships, etc. In this paper, we integrate the users' similarity and trust into our prediction model based on user-based collaborative filtering.

3   Methods

3.1   Computing Interest Based on Similarity

As the Fig. 2 shown, we regard the tweet as the item and calculate the users' similarity by the users-tweets ratings matrix based on the user-based collaborative filtering. The ratings matrix only contains 0 and 1. Retweeting a tweet corresponds to a 1 rating, not-retweeting to a 0 rating. Table 1 shows the users-tweets ratings matrix.

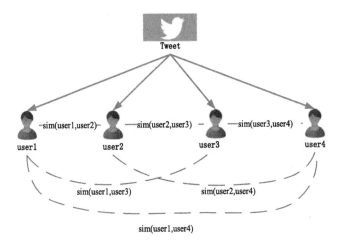

Fig. 2. Similarity between users who retweeted the same tweet

After getting the users-tweets ratings matrix, given a user u and a tweet t, the predicted interest value that u retweet t is calculated as below:

Table 1. Users-tweets ratings matrix

	Tweet 1	...	Tweet j	...	Tweet n
User 1	r_{11}	...	r_{1j}	...	r_{1n}
...	...	...	...	...	...
User i	r_{i1}	...	r_{ij}	...	r_{in}
...	...	...	...	...	...
User m	r_{m1}	...	r_{mj}	...	r_{mn}

$$p(u,t) = \sum_{v \in S(u,K) \cap N(t)} sim(u,v) r_{vt} \tag{1}$$

Here $S(u, K)$ contains most similar K users with the user u, $N(t)$ indicates users who retweet the tweet t. r_{vt} is whether the user v retweet the tweet t (1 for yes, 0 for no). $sim(u, v)$ is the similarity between the user u and the user v,it is the key step in the user-based collaborative filtering and has an important impact on the algorithm results. The $sim(u, v)$ is caculated by using the IUF(Inverse User Frequence) [6]:

$$sim(u,v) = \frac{\sum\limits_{i \in N(u) \cap N(v)} \frac{1}{\log(1+retweetCount(i))}}{\sqrt{|N(u)||N(v)|}} \tag{2}$$

Here, $N(u)$ is tweets that the user u retweeted, $N(v)$ is tweets that the user v retweeted. $retweetCount(i)$ is times which tweet i is retweeted. $\frac{1}{\ln(1+retweetCount(i))}$ is the penalty factor [7]. The more the tweet is retweeted, the less its value is. The denominator is the regularization term, which scales the value from 0 to 1.

Then we can get the similarity matrix W from the $sim(u, v)$:

$$W_{similarity} = \begin{bmatrix} w_{11} & w_{12} & ... & w_{1m} \\ w_{21} & w_{22} & ... & w_{2m} \\ ... & ... & ... & ... \\ w_{m1} & w_{m2} & ... & w_{mm} \end{bmatrix} \tag{3}$$

3.2   Computing Interest Based on Trust

However, unlike the stuff purchasing, tweets' retweeting behaviors spread like a tree shown in Fig. 3. So we introduce the trust feature to build our collaborative model. The trust feature means that if the user v retweet a tweet the user u post, then we believe that the user v is trust in the user u. For evaluation, we make an assumption below:

Assumption. Tweet retweeted time by the user v closer the published time by the user u, the higher trust degree that the user v to the user u.

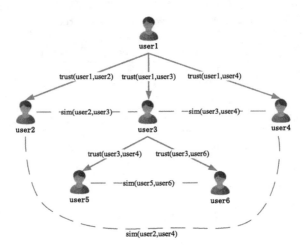

Fig. 3. Similarity between users who retweet same tweet

Intuitively, if the user u post a tweet k and the user v retweets the tweet k, it means that the user v like the tweet k and will like to share this tweet with his followers. It also means the user v trusted the user u. The more quickly retweeting time to the post time, the more attention the user v pays to the user u. Then we introduce the negative exponential distribution to simulate the delay between retweeted time and post time:

$$trust_k(x; \lambda) = \begin{cases} \lambda e^{-\lambda x} & x \geq 0 \\ 0 & x < 0 \end{cases} \tag{4}$$

Here x is calculated as below:

$$x = \frac{createdAt_{user_u}(k) - createdAt_{user_v}(k)}{createdAt_{max}(k) - createdAt_{min}(k)} \text{(if u,v are adjacent)} \tag{5}$$

Where $createdAt_{user_u}(k) - createdAt_{user_v}(k)$ refers to the delay between the $user_u$ retweeted tweet and the time $user_v$ post the tweet. $createdAt_{max}(k) - createdAt_{min}(k)$ measures the max tweet's delay between latest retweeted time and original post time.

The maximum likelihood estimate for the rate parameter λ is:

$$\widehat{\lambda} = \frac{1}{\bar{x}} \tag{6}$$

where: $\bar{x} = \frac{1}{n} \sum_{i=1}^{n} x_i$ is the sample mean.

Meanwhile, trust can transfer. It means if the user w retweets the tweet k which the user u retweet by the user v, the trust that the user w to the user v calculated as follow:

$$Path_k(user_w, user_v) = \{trust_1(w, u), trust_2(u, v)\} \tag{7}$$

$$trust_k(user_w, user_v) = \prod_{i \in S(user_w, user_v)} trust_i \tag{8}$$

Here, the Eq. (7) is the retweeting route from w to v, which contains the trust value between w and v. Eq. (8) is the product of trust value in $Path_k(user_w, user_v)$.

According to the one-tweet's trust, the trust that the user w to the user v calculated as follow:

$$trust(user_w, user_v) = \sum_{k=1}^{m} trust_k \tag{9}$$

Then we can get the trust matrix based on trust.

$$W_{trust} = \begin{bmatrix} w_{11} & w_{12} & \cdots & w_{1m} \\ w_{21} & w_{22} & \cdots & w_{2m} \\ \cdots & \cdots & \cdots & \cdots \\ w_{m1} & w_{m2} & \cdots & w_{mm} \end{bmatrix} \tag{10}$$

According to the trust feature, we can caculate the interest value if given a user and a tweet:

$$p(u, t) = \sum_{v \in S(u,K) \cap N(t)} trust(u, v) r_{vt} \tag{11}$$

The Eq. (11) is almost the same as the Eq. (1). It means the interest that the user u to the tweet t which the user v post.

3.3 Computing Interest Based on Similarities and Trust

According to the previous description, we conclude two predict interest formulas according to the similarity and trust as follow:

$$p_{sim}(u, t) = \sum_{v \in S(u,K) \cap N(t)} sim(u, v) r_{vt} \tag{12}$$

$$p_{trust}(u, t) = \sum_{v \in S(u,K) \cap N(t)} trust(u, v) r_{vt} \tag{13}$$

The two equations both can be interpreted as the preference of the user u to tweet t. To adapt the scenario of retweeting behaviors, we modify the user-based collaborative filtering model by integrating the trust feature. Then we propose a new predict interest formula based on the $p_{sim}(u, t)$ and the $p_{trust}(u, t)$ by normalizing respectively:

$$p_{interest}(u, t) = \alpha \|p_{trust}(u, t)\| + (1 - \alpha)\|p_{sim}(u, t)\| \tag{14}$$

where α is the weighted parameter valued between 0 and 1. Then the algorithm updates the parameter α and loops over the test dataset. The effectiveness of algorithm is discussed in Sect. 4.

4   Experimental Studies

In this section, we describe our datasets and the preprocessing steps followed by the experimental results for each step in our model.

4.1   Dataset

Using Twitter's API, we crawled over 10 thousand users and 80 million tweets. we randomly selected users and expanded the user base by following their followers' and followees' links. After following several steps of links, we got over 10 thousands users and collected the tweets they had posted in a four months period from March 2014 to June 2014.

4.2   Preprocessing

In order to better close to real behaviors of users. Firstly we divided the crawled tweets into 4 parts by month and got the 4 parts of one-month dataset.

Then considering the effectiveness of algorithm, we preprocessed the one-month dataset according to the following criteria:

- Users should have retweet at least 10 tweets in order to ensure that they are relatively active.
- In order to get the retweeting information, tweets should have been retweeted.

As there is no API to directly get followees' tweets for each user without authorization. The only way to get users' scanned tweets is to simulate the timeline of a user, we collected users who have over fifteen followees in our one-month dataset and regarded tweets posted by followees in the one-month dataset as scanned tweets of users. Then we sorted scanned tweets of each user in chronological order. Finally we obtained simulated scanned tweets set of each user. The first three-fourths of simulated scanned tweets set of each user was put in the training set and others in the test set. Table 2 shows the number of tweets and users in the training set and test set of each month.

We used the retweeted tweets of each user in the training set to build the similarity matrix and trust matrix and predicted the retweeted tweets of each user in the test set based on similarity matrix and trust matrix.

4.3   Evaluation Metrics

We compute the mean average precision (MAP) to evaluate the proposed approach. For a given user, average precision (AP) is defined as:

$$AP = \frac{\sum_{r=1}^{N} p(r) \times rel(r)}{|R|} \tag{15}$$

Table 2. Training dataset and test dataset

Time	Training set	Test set
2014.03	users:6279 tweets:52746	users:6279 tweets:17581
2014.04	users:8327 tweets:121630	users:8327 tweets:40543
2014.05	users:5732 tweets:64367	users:5732 tweets:21455
2014.06	users:5437 tweets:40620	users:5437 tweets:13540

Where r is the number of scanned tweets for a given user; $|R|$ is the number of retweeted tweets for a given user; $rel(r)$ is a binary function to describe whether the user has retweeted the tweet in the scanned tweet list.

Then the MAP can be obtained by averaging the AP values of all the users:

$$MAP = \frac{\sum_{j=1}^{m} AP_j}{m} \qquad (16)$$

4.4 Method Comparison and Result Discussion

The Fig. 4 presents our proposed approach results of MAP by adjust the model parameter *alpha*. We find that our proposed method can get the best result

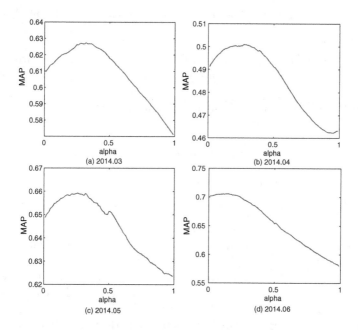

Fig. 4. Method comparison

Table 3. Comparsion of the two methods based on map (%)

Time	2014.03	2014.04	2014.05	2014.06
SBM	61.91	48.93	64.78	69.87
TBM	57.46	43.41	57.42	53.99
Our method	62.74	50.10	65.93	70.57

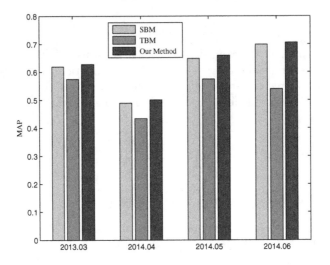

Fig. 5. The MAP value of our proposed method based on different alpha

when parameter is between the 0.2 and 0.3. That means the similarity feature is more userful than the trust feature to present the users' personal interest in our dataset.

In order to discover more result details based on similarity and trust, We compared with following methods:

– Similarity-Based Method (SBM): The traditional collaborative filtering based on users' similarity.
– Trust-Based Method (TBM): Only based on the users' trust to predict retweeting behaviors.

By using our proposed method which select the best weighted parameter and compared methods to process our dataset, we obtain following results, as shown in Fig. 5 and Table 3.

According to the Fig. 5 and the Table 3, our proposed method averagely exhibits higher MAP by 9.26 % and 0.96 % than the Trust-Based Method and the Similarity-Based Method on the each month of dataset, respectively. The results show Similarity-Based Method has better performance than Trust-Based Method on our dataset. However, according to AP results of each month's test set, we found the Trust-Based Method have higher AP value than the Similarity-Based Method on some users' data. Analyzing their retweeted tweets which our method predicted, we found among these users, most users are fans of musical stars or movie stars in the real world and they followed these stars on twitter. They retweet tweets of their favorite stars frequently. So the value of weighted parameter in our model depend on the proportion of stars' fans in our dataset. The higher the ratio, the bigger the weighted parameter.

For the limitations of our method, which doesn't analyze the text of tweets, caculating the weighted parameter and users' ratio is a diffcult part in our research. To improve our method's accuracy, this will be the key point of our next research.

5 Conclusion and Future Work

In this paper, we propose a new collaborative model to predict retweeting behaviors. Our approach takes advantage of user-based collaborative filtering by collecting retweeting behaviors. Moreover, we incorporate the users' trust into our model to improve the effectiveness of the algorithm. Our experiments with real-life dataset have demonstrated the effectiveness in retweeting behaviors prediction.

Some future research directions are as follows. First, through analyzing of our dataset, we find that spreading information by retweeting is not complete and it can weak the effectiveness of the algorithm by calculating the users' trust and similarity. This happens due to the lack of data collection, so we must upgrade twitter crawler. Then the cold-start is another important issue to deal with. Our model doesn't consider the new users and tweets. To address this problem, we consider to detect the users' interest by using some text mining algorithms on tweets and incorporating the users' social relationship.

Acknowledgments. The research is supported by National Natural Science Foundation of China (No. 71331008).

References

1. Chen, K., Chen, T., Zheng, G., Jin, O., Yao, E., Yu, Y.: Collaborative personalized tweet recommendation. In: Proceedings of the 35th International ACM SIGIR Conference on Research and Development in Information Rretrieval, pp. 661–670. ACM (2012)
2. Yang, Z., Guo, J., Cai, K., Tang, J., Li, J., Zhang, L., Su, Z.: Understanding retweeting behaviors in social networks. In: Proceedings of the 19th ACM International Conference on Information and Knowledge Management, pp. 1633–1636. ACM (2010)
3. Chen, J., Nairn, R., Nelson, L., Bernstein, M., Chi, E.: Short and tweet: experiments on recommending content from information streams. In: Proceedings of the SIGCHI Conference on Human Factors in Computing Systems, pp. 1185–1194. ACM (2010)

4. Volkovs, M., Zemel, R. S.: Collaborative ranking with 17 parameters. In: Advances in Neural Information Processing Systems, pp. 2294–2302 (2012)
5. Yuan, Q., Chen, L., Zhao, S.: Factorization vs. regularization: fusing heterogeneous social relationships in top-n recommendation. In: Proceedings of the Fifth ACM Conference on Recommender Systems, pp. 245–252. ACM (2011)
6. Uysal, I., Croft, W. B.: User oriented tweet ranking: a filtering approach to microblogs. In: Proceedings of the 20th ACM International Conference on Information and Knowledge Management, pp. 2261–2264. ACM (2011)
7. Breese, J.S., Heckerman, D., Kadie, C.: Empirical analysis of predictive algorithms for collaborative filtering. In: Proceedings of the Fourteenth Conference on Uncertainty in Artificial Intelligence, pp. 43–52. Morgan Kaufmann Publishers Inc., San Francisco (1998)

Protecting Location Privacy in Spatial Crowdsourcing

Jie Hu[1,2]($\boxtimes$), Liusheng Huang[1,2], Lu Li[1,2], Mingyu Qi[2], and Wei Yang[1,2]

[1] School of Computer Science and Technology,
University of Science and Technology of China,
Hefei, Anhui, People's Republic of China
[2] Suzhou Institute for Advanced Study,
University of Science and Technology of China,
Suzhou, Jiangsu, People's Republic of China
{hujie826,liluzq,sa614405}@mail.ustc.edu.cn, {lshuang,qubit}@ustc.edu.cn

Abstract. Recently, spatial crowdsourcing has attracted wide attention in both the research community and industry, one of which is the eMarket platform. It enables requesters to release *spatial tasks* (i.e., tasks related to a location) and expect them to be performed by *workers* (i.e., users with smart mobile devices). One of the key functions of such platform is spatial tasks assignment. The traditional solutions to the tasks assignment problem require workers to disclose their locations to the spatial crowdsourcing server (SC-server), which are untrustworthy entities. In this paper, we employ the peer-to-peer spatial K-anonymity to protect the workers' location privacy. However, it will result in the consequence that various spatial tasks can't be performed. To improve the spatial task assignment, we propose an optimized scheme for spatial task assignment without compromising the workers' location privacy, and verify the effect through our experiments.

Keywords: Spatial crowdsourcing · Location privacy · Spatial K-anonymity · Spatial task assignment

1 Introduction

With the development of smart mobile devices, users with it could easily collect and share various types of data (e.g., picture, video, audio, location, time). Exploiting this phenomena, a new platform for efficient and scalable data collection has emerged, which is called *Spatial Crowdsourcing* (SC). The spatial crowdsourcing enables subscribers to publish tasks with specific space and time attributes on the platform and the workers (with smart mobile devices) can perform the tasks if they are at the right time and at the right place. It recently received wide attention (e.g., [13,28,29] *etc.*). Based on the difference of spatial task assignment modes, spatial crowdsourcing can be classified into two categories [1]: *Worker Selected Tasks*(WST) and *Server Assigned Tasks*(SAT).

© Springer International Publishing Switzerland 2015
R. Cai et al. (Eds.): APWeb 2015 Workshops, LNCS 9461, pp. 113–124, 2015.
DOI: 10.1007/978-3-319-28121-6_11

In WST mode, online workers can choose any spatial tasks in their spatial region (the area in which the worker can accept spatial task) to perform without coordinating with SC-server. One advantage of this mode is that the workers need not worry about the threat of their location privacy since they don't reveal their location to SC-server. But this may result that some tasks get assigned many times while others have never been performed. It is always sub-optimal when the tasks are assigned since the workers don't have a global system view. Different from the WST mode, the SC-server will collect the location information of all the online workers, and give the assignment scheme based on global optimization in SAT mode. This is desired. However, it will pose threat to the workers' location privacy since the SC-server are untrustworthy entities.

To address this problem, To *et al.* present the first secure framework in spatial crowdsourcing [2]. They employ the differential private spatial decompositions approach to ensure that the SC-server will not get the sensitive information about the workers. However, they don't consider the spatial region for each worker, i.e., each worker in their system could travel everywhere. To remedy this defect, Pournajaf *et al.* present spatial task assignment with cloaking area [16]. They assume that each worker has a limited travel budget. Nevertheless, they refer to the workers' cloaking area as their spatial region, which will leak much location information of the workers.

In this paper, we focus on SAT mode. There are two constraints for the worker to perform the spatial tasks: the spatial region R and $maxT$ (the maximum number of tasks that the worker is willing to perform). The optimization goal of spatial crowdsourcing is to maximize the overall task assignment while conforming to the constraints of the workers. This problem is called *maximum task assignment (MTA)* problem. To satisfy the workers' requirement of the privacy, we employ the peer-to-peer spatial K-anonymity (SKA) technology [5]. In this way, each worker is cloaked among other K-1 workers. Moreover, everyone has a cloaking area. Then the new challenges will arise. While the workers regard their cloaking area as their spatial region, much more overlapped region exists in the cloaking area. That will cost much more computation and communication resources. On the other hand, some workers' spatial regions may be contained by more than one cloaking area. Then how to assign the worker's $maxT$ to those cloaking areas is another challenge.

The main contributions of this paper can be summarized as:

- To reduce the computation and communication overhead, we employ a greedy algorithm to select minimum cloaking area to cover all the workers' spatial regions.
- We introduce a new parameter to address the problem of the $maxT$ assignment. Based on the parameter, we propose an assignment algorithm to assign the $maxT$.
- We analyze the security strength and privacy-preservation ability of the approach and analyze the complexity of $maxT$ assignment algorithm.
- We conduct an extensive set of experiments on real and synthetic datasets to evaluate the performance without compromising the workers' location privacy.

The remainder of the paper is organized as follows. In Sect. 2, we discuss literature relevant to our work. Next we discuss some background studies, and then formally define our problem and the system model in Sect. 3. Thereafter we explain our approach in Sect. 4. Section 5 reports the experiment results. Finally, in Sect. 6 we conclude our study and prospect for the future work.

2   Related Work

Much work has been done on crowdsourcing [10–12,17]. It also has been applied in the industry (e.g., MTurk, CrowFlower and oDesk). Spatial crowdsourcing as a special class of the crowdsourcing was proposed recently [7,14]. Kazemi *et al.* introduced a framework for maximizing the number of assigned tasks [1], and they reduced the MAT problem to the maximum flow problem. Deng *et al.* study a version of the spatial crowdsourcing problem in which the workers autonomously select their tasks [15]. They aim to find a schedule for the worker that maximizes the number of performed tasks, which is NP-hard.

Location privacy has received widely attention over recent years [8,19–24]. The traditional techniques for location privacy are location perturbation and obfuscation, which have been widely used. Gruteser *et al.* introduce the K-anonymity into location privacy [9], where the location of a user is hidden among other K users. But it may lead to a single point of attack. To sidestep this problem, much work focuses on peer-to-peer anonymization [18].

While much work has done in location privacy, only few work focused on location privacy for spatial crowdsourcing [2,16,27]. To *et al.* focus on the SAT mode and employ the differential private spatial decompositions approach [2]. However, they ignore the spatial region for each worker. Pournajaf *et al.* suggest that each worker has a limited travel budget [16] when assigning spatial task with cloaking area. Nevertheless, they refer to the workers' cloaking area as their spatial region. It may not satisfy some workers' requirements of the privacy. In contrast, the workers could require the cloaking area by themselves.

3   Preliminaries

We introduce the *spatial K-anonymity* (SKA) in Sect. 3.1. Section 3.2 presents the formal problem definition and system model.

3.1   Spatial K-anonymity

Spatial K-anonymity (SKA) is a spatial cloaking technique that the location of the worker is cloaked among the other $K-1$ workers. The main idea of the peer-to-peer SKA approach (see [5]) is that a worker communicates with his neighboring peers via multi-hop routing to find at least other $K-1$ peers. Each worker has their own privacy requirements for the cloaked area contains at least K workers, and minimum area A_{min}. i.e., the size of a cloaked area is at least A_{min}. Figure 1 shows an example of the peer-to-peer spatial cloaking, where $\{m_6, m_7, m_9, m_{10}, m_{11}\}$ (the black disc) is to blur the identity of m_8 (the black triangle), and the rectangular region is to cloak the location of m_8. All the workers to blur the worker m_8 must distribute in the cloaked area. So the K that worker m_8 requires is no more than 6, and the minimum cloaked area A_{min} is in the solid lined rectangle.

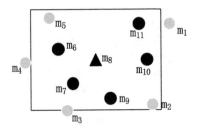 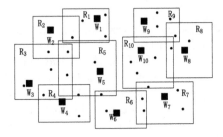

Fig. 1. Example of the peer-to-peer spatial cloaking

Fig. 2. Illustrating an example of SC

3.2 Formal Problem Definition and System Model

We consider the spatial crowdsourcing task assignment in the SAT mode first, i.e., workers send their location to the SC-server. After the SC-server receiving the location of all the workers, it assigns the task to every worker. As is shown in Fig. 2, the worker is a carrier of a mobile device to perform spatial tasks. We describe the worker and spatial tasks as follows.

- **Worker**: A worker W_i is a carrier of a mobile device who volunteers to perform spatial tasks. The form of workers' constraints is defined as $<R_i, maxT_i>$, where R_i is the spatial region in which the worker can accept spatial tasks. $maxT_i$ is the maximum number of spatial tasks that the worker is willing to perform.
- **Spatial Task**: The spatial task t is related to location and form as $< l >$, where l is the location information of the task.

We suggest that every spatial task be performed only once in this paper. For the task that needs to be performed k times, we could transform it into k tasks that only need to be performed once.

As required, workers trust each other, and don't reveal any sensitive information of their peers. But they trust neither the SC-server nor the requesters. While some workers' location information has been known to the adversary, it should not pose a threat to the system if the system can successfully disassociate the queries from their locations.

Figure 3 shows the system architecture. Workers first employ the peer-to-peer SKA method to cloak their location and identity. We assume the worker's

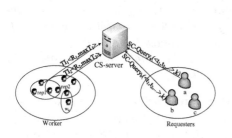

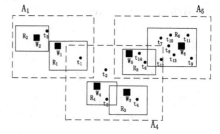

Fig. 3. System model of SC

Fig. 4. Cloaking area and the task assignment.

cloaking area contains his spatial region (if it is not, combine his spatial region with his cloaking area as his new cloaking area). Then some workers' spatial region may be contained by other workers' cloaking area. As it is shown in Fig. 4, the worker W_i associated with spatial region R_i (the solid rectangular region). The cloaking area A_4 (the dashed rectangular region) is to cloak the worker W_4, and R_5 is contained by A_4. Considering that the valid region of cloaking area is in the spatial region, we ignore the region that is out of the spatial region in the cloaking area. When A_i contains the spatial region $R_{i_1}, R_{i_2}, \cdots, R_{i_{k_i}}$, it can be denoted by a set $A_i = \{R_{i_1}, R_{i_2}, \cdots, R_{i_{k_i}}\}$. Then, worker W_i employs the PiRi technology to select the representative spatial region from A_i.

However, much more overlapped region exists in the cloaking area when we take it as the spatial region, and much region in the cloaking area is invalid. That will cost much more computation and communication resources. On the other hand, some workers' spatial region may be contained by more than one workers' cloaking area. Then the problem is how to assign the worker's $maxT$ to those cloaking area. As Fig. 4 illustrates. The maximum number of acceptable tasks for worker W_i is $maxT_i$. As the spatial region R_5 is contained by both A_4 and A_5, then how to assigned the $maxT_5$ to A_4 and A_5. In the following, we will solve this problem.

4   Privacy Preserving Approach for Task Assignment

In this section, we first select minimum cloaking area to cover all the workers' spatial regions. Next, we pose an assignment algorithm to assign the $maxT$.

4.1   Cloaking Area Selection

To reduce the computation and communication overhead, instead of sending all the workers' cloaking areas to the SC-server, we only select some of them which could cover all the workers' spatial regions. Then, the problem is how to select the cloaking areas. To address this problem, we should solve the following optimization problem.

Definition 1 (V-Cover). *Giving a set of workers W, each worker has his spatial region and cloaking area. The cloaking area contains his spatial region. Set R denotes the workers' spatial region, and set A denotes their cloaking area. The V-Cover problem is to finds a subset $A' \subseteq A$ such that the subset covers the region of entire set R with minimum cardinality.*

Definition 2 (Minimum Set Cover Problem). *Let $U = \{u_1, u_2, u_3, \cdots, u_n\}$ be a collection of finite sets. $S = \{S_1, S_2, S_3, \cdots, S_k\}$ is subsets of U. Their elements are drawn from a universal set U, i.e., $S_i \subseteq U$ and $\bigcup_{i=1}^{k} S_i = U$. Minimum set cover finds a set $C \subseteq S$ with minimum cardinality where $\bigcup_{S_i \in C} S_i = U$.*

Leyla *et al.*, has proven that the V-Cover problem is NP-hard by reducing from the minimum set cover problem [3]. To get an approximation solution, we employ the greedy algorithm which is based on the following heuristic: at each stage of the algorithm, pick the set with the largest number of uncovered elements [25]. Consequently, in order to address the V-Cover problem, during each step of the algorithm, we should select a representative worker whose cloaking area covers the largest number of uncovered spatial region from R.

4.2 The $maxT$ Assignment

If these selected cloaking areas have no overlapped area. The maximum number of acceptable tasks $maxT$ for each cloaking area is the summation of all the workers' $maxT$ that their spatial regions are contained by the cloaking area. But it is not always this case. As it is shown in Fig. 4, the selected cloaking area is $\{A_1, A_4, A_5\}$. The maximum number of acceptable tasks for cloaking area A_i is denoted by $maxT_{A_i}$. Then $maxT_{A_1} = maxT_1 + maxT_2$. However, the spatial region R_5 is contained by both A_4 and A_5. So the problem is how to assign $maxT_5$ to those cloaking areas. We will address it in the following.

Definition 3 (Task Density). *Task density, denoted by TD, refers to average number of tasks in a spatial region for a fixed time. It can be inferred from previous experience.*

There are different TD in different spatial regions. As Fig. 4 illustrates, there are many tasks in the spatial region R_6, but less in other spatial regions. If $maxT_6$ is small, there will be many tasks in R_6 which can't be completed. As we add the $maxT_5$ to A_5, the SC-server may assign more tasks to A_5, but many of them in R_6. That will make more tasks can't be performed. Here, we introduce a new parameter Er. The task density of R_i is denoted by TD_i. For worker W_i, $Er_i = maxT_i - TD_i$. We can simply infer that if $Er_i \geq 0$, then all the tasks in R_i can be performed by W_i. Otherwise, at least $(-Er_i)$ tasks in R_i can't be performed. For each cloaking area, Er_{A_i} is the summation of all the Er_j that the R_j is only contained by A_i. i.e., $Er_{A_i} = \sum_{R_j ! \in A_i} Er_j$. ($R_j ! \in A_i$ refers that R_j is contained and only contained by A_i).

The pseudocode of the $maxT$ assignment is described in Algorithm 1. ER_i is the set of the Er_{A_j} that A_j contains R_i. The algorithm first judges whether the

---

Algorithm 1. $maxT_i$ assignment

1: CA_i=set of cloaking area that contain spatial regions R_i;
2: $n_i=|CA_i|$;
3: ER_i=set of the Er_{A_j} that $A_j \in CA_i$;
4: **if** $n_i=1$ **then**
5:    $maxT_i$ is assigned to the only area in set CA_i;
6: **else**
7:    **if** $\max\{ER_i\} <= 0$ **then**
8:       MEA=the set of cloaking area A_m s.t. $Er_{A_m}=\max\{ER_i\}$;
9:       Equal distribute the $maxT_i$ to those cloaking areas in MEA;
10:    **else**
11:       NEA=the set of cloaking area A_n that $Er_{A_n}>0$;
12:       $sum=\sum_{A_n \in NEA} Er_{A_n}$;
13:       **for** each $A_j \in NEA$ **do**
14:          Assign $\left\lceil \frac{Er_{A_j}}{sum} \times maxT_i \right\rceil$ to A_j;
15:       **end for**
16:    **end if**
17: **end if**

---

maximum value in ER_i is greater than 0. If it is not, we select the cloaking areas with maximum Er in set ER_i and equally distribute $maxT_i$ to those cloaking areas. Otherwise, for all the cloaking areas that their Er is greater than 0, based on their value of the Er, it will assign the $maxT_i$ to those cloaking areas on a pro rata.

To explain the details of the assignment mechanism, we will give an example in the following. As Fig. 2 illustrates, the information of each worker is shown in Table 1. Suggest the final selected cloaking areas are $\{A_1, A_3, A_4, A_5, A_8\}$, and $A_3 \cap A_4 = R_4$, $A_3 \cap A_5 = R_5$. Then we will assign the $maxT_4$ to A_3 and A_4, and assign the $maxT_5$ to A_3 and A_5. As we can learn from Fig. 2, $Er_{A_3} = Er_3 = 5$, $Er_{A_4} = Er_6 + Er_7 = 3$, $Er_{A_5} = Er_{10} = -4$. Since $Er_{A_3} > 0$ and $Er_{A_4} > 0$. For the $maxT_4$, we will assign the value

$$\left\lceil maxT_4 \times \frac{Er_{A_3}}{Er_{A_3} + Er_{A_4}} \right\rceil = 6$$

to A_3, and the value

$$\left\lceil maxT_4 \times \frac{Er_{A_4}}{Er_{A_3} + Er_{A_4}} \right\rceil = 4$$

to A_4. As $Er_{A_5} < 0$ and $Er_{A_3} > 0$. The $maxT_5$ will be assigned to A_3.

For each of the cloaking area that has been selected, instead of the worker who owns the cloaking area to send it to the SC-server, we employ PiRi [3] approach to select a representative in the cloaking area to do it. Since Kazemi,L et al. proposed an attack model while the workers sended the cloaking area by themselves [3]. As the MTA problem could be reduced to the maximum flow problem [1], after the SC-server receives all the cloaking area, the SC-server

Table 1. Illustration of the $maxT$ and Er

Worker	W_1	W_2	W_3	W_4	W_5	W_6	W_7	W_8	W_9	W_{10}
$maxT$	10	8	10	9	2	5	10	8	6	3
Task Densities	1	6	5	7	8	8	4	7	2	7
Er	9	2	5	2	−6	−3	6	1	4	−4

employs Ford-Fulkerson algorithm [4] to assign the task to every representative. When the representative receives the task from the SC-server, he will employ Geocast approach [6] to send the message to all the workers that whose spatial region is contained in the cloaking area he stand for. Then workers will select the task by themselves.

4.3   Analysis

Security and Privacy Analysis: In this paper, we employ the peer-to-peer spatial K-anonymity and PiRi techniques to protect the workers' location privacy. For the P2P SKA approach, the cloaking area satisfies the worker's K-anonymity and minimum area privacy requirements. Worker blurs his location among the other $K - 1$ workers, such that the probability of identifying the worker's identity does not exceed $1/K$, even in the worst case when all the worker locations are known to the adversary.

As the cloaking areas sent by workers have significant overlaps, which may reveal extra information to the server as compared to the conventional location-based attacks, introduce major privacy leaks to the system. While we employ the PiRi approach and it is 98 % more resilient to location-based attacks by the experiments [3].

Time Complexity: The time complexity of our $maxT$ assignment method is $O(n)$ where n is the number of workers. Algorithm 1 runs no more than n rounds, so the time complexity of whole process of the $maxT$ assignment is $O(n^2)$.

5   Performance Evaluation

In this section, we conducted experimentally with both real and synthetic datasets to evaluate the performance of our method. In the following section, we first discuss the method of our experimentally, then present the results and analyze it.

5.1   Experimental Methodology

We obtain the real data from Gowalla [26], a location-based social network, where users are able to check in to different spots in their vicinity. The check-ins include the time and location information. We use check-in data over a period of one year, i.e., 2010. In the state of Missouri, we assume that the Gowalla users are the workers in the spatial crowdsourcing system and their $maxT$ is the number of their check-ins in that year. We suppose the minimum boundary rectangle of each worker' checked-in locations as their spatial region R.

We randomly generate data from a uniform distribution for spatial tasks. Worker can accept spatial task if it is in his spatial region. All the workers' privacy requirement K level varies in the rang [5,19]. The minimum area requirement is set to zero in all cases. The current location of each worker is the centre of his spatial region. For worker W_i, if his requirement of K-anonymity level is K_i, then he selects the nearest K_i-1 workers to blur his identity. To evaluate the performance of our method, we compare it with randomly assigning the $maxT$ to those cloaking areas.

The number of tasks in all of our experiments is varied between 1000 to 5000. The latitude interval increases from 0.5 to 2.0 and so as the longitude. We will increase the time interval of experiment data from one month to one year. Finally, for each of our experiments, we run 10 cases, and report the average of the results.

5.2   Experiment Results

In this subsection, we report the results of our experiments and then analyze it. In the first experiment, we evaluate the performance of our method by varying the number of spatial tasks from 1000 to 5000. The number of workers is 3368. We select 67 cloaking areas when employing the selecting algorithm which can reduce the computation expense and communication overhead. The result is shown in Fig. 5.

Figure 5(a) depicts the number of the tasks accomplished with different methods. The assignment can achieve optimal performance without considering the workers' location privacy, which is denoted by **optimal** in the figure. **SAM** approach is to employ our $maxT$ assignment algorithm. The **SRM** approach is to randomly assign the $maxT$ to those cloaking areas. We compare SAM with SRM. Intuitively, we can learn that SAM could perform more tasks than SRM. As the location privacy, it will reduce the number of tasks accomplished. We evaluate the performance of one approach as follows:

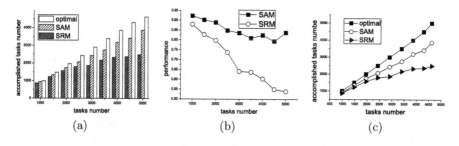

Fig. 5. The performance of tasks accomplished.

$$performance = \frac{|approach|}{|optimal|}$$

$|approach|$ means that the number of tasks that the approach (SAM or SRM) accomplishes. $|optimal|$ means that the number of tasks that optimal approach accomplishes.

We can learn the performance of all the methods from Fig. 5(b). The performance of SAM can reach 70%–90%, while the SRM can only reach 50%–70%. As the number of spatial tasks increases, the performance of the SAM changed relatively little, but the performance of SRM constantly reduce. So the SAM has the obvious advantage when the number of tasks is large. Figure 5(c) shows the trends of the number of accomplished tasks by SAM, SRM and optimal.

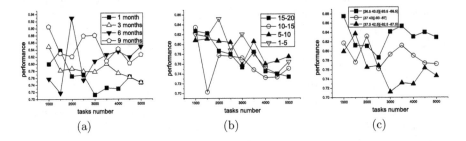

Fig. 6. Impact on performance of SAM. (a) is the time impacts on the performance. (b) is the K-anonymity level impacts on the performance. (c) is the size of the spatial region impacts on the performance.

Figure 6 shows the different factor impacts on the performance of SAM. Figure 6(a) depicts the time impacts on the performance. We increase the time from one month to nine months. Then the number of workers in the spatial region will also increase. The average of the performance is improved as the time last long. For 9 months, the average of the performance is 84%, while it is only 81% for 6 months. And the other statistics are 78% for 3 months as well as 76% for one month. As time changed ,the only changed factor is the number of the workers. The longer the time duration, the more workers take part in. So the performance of SAM will improve when the number of the workers increases.

Figure 6(b) depicts the K-anonymity level impacts on the performance. The average performance is 77% when the K-anonymity levels is in 15–20 while it is 75% when the K-anonymity levels is in 10–15, and 78% when in 5–10, 79% when in 1–5. It can be seen that the influence of the K-anonymity level to the performance is not significant. To improve the security, we can improve the K-anonymity level for every worker.

Figure 6(c) depicts the size of the spatial region impacts on the performance. It can be seen from the figure, the bigger size of the spatial region, the better performance of SAM. When the latitude and longitude interval are [36.5 43.5] and [-93.5 -86.5], the average performance is 83 %. But it is only 76 % when they are [37.5 42.5] and [-92.5 -87.5].

From the above experiments, we can learn that in the same spatial region, the more workers, the better performance. And for the same number of tasks, the bigger spatial region, the better performance.

6 Conclusion and Future Work

In this paper, we employ the peer-to-peer spatial K-anonymity approach to protect the workers' location privacy in SAT mode of the spatial crowdsourcing. To accomplish more tasks, we proposed a selecting algorithm and $maxT$ assignment algorithm, which can achieve an optimal result without compromising their location privacy. With our experiments, we demonstrate the effectiveness of our approach.

As future work, we will consider the different types of task, and each worker can only accept certain types of task. In that case, we will consider a new method to assign the tasks without compromising the workers' location privacy.

References

1. Kazemi, L., Shahabi, C.: Geocrowd: enabling query answering with spatial crowdsourcing. In: ACM SIGSPATIAL GIS 2012, pp. 189–198 (2012)
2. To, H., Ghinita, G., Shahabi, C.: A framework for protecting worker location privacy in spatial crowdsourcing. In: International Conference on Very Large Data Bases (VLDB), Hangzhou, China (2014)
3. Kazemi, L., Shahabi, C.: A privacy-aware framework for participatory sensing. SIGKDD Explor. **13**(1), 45–51 (2011)
4. Kleinberg, J., Tardos, E.: Algorithm Design. Addison-Wesley Longman Publishing Co. Inc., Boston (2005)
5. Chow, C.Y., Mokbel, M.F., Liu, X.: Spatial cloaking for anonymous location-based services in mobile peer-to-peer environments. GeoInformatica **15**(2), 351–380 (2011)
6. Navas, J.C., Imielinski, T.: Geocastgeographic addressing and routing. In: International Conference on Mobile Computing and Networking (MOBICOM), pp. 66–76 (1997)
7. Alt, F., Shirazi, A.S., Schmidt, A., Kramer, U., Nawaz, Z.: Location-based crowdsourcing: extending crowdsourcing to the real world. In: International Conference on Human-Computer Interaction (NordiCHI), pp. 13–22 (2010)
8. Niu, B., Li, Q., Zhu, X., Cao, G., Li, H.: Achieving k-anonymity in privacy-aware location-based services. In: International Conference on INFOCOM. IEEE (2014)
9. Gruteser, M., Grunwald, D.: Anonymous usage of location-based services through spatial and temporal cloaking. In: International Conference on Mobile Systems, Applications and Services, pp. 31–42. ACM (2003)
10. Hirth, M., Scheuring, S., Hossfeld, T., et al.: Predicting result quality in crowdsourcing using application layer monitoring. In: International Conference on Communications and Electronics (ICCE), pp. 510–515. IEEE (2014)

11. Horton, J.J., Chilton, L.B.: The labor economics of paid crowdsourcing. In: International Conference on Electronic Commerce, pp. 209–218. ACM (2010)
12. Poetz, M.K., Schreier, M.: The value of crowdsourcing: can users really compete with professionals in generating new product ideas? J. Prod. Innov. Manage. **29**(2), 245–256 (2012)
13. Dang, H., Nguyen, T., To, H.: Maximum complex task assignment: towards tasks correlation in spatial crowdsourcing. In: International Conference on Information Integration and Web-based Applications & Services. ACM (2013)
14. Kazemi, L., Shahabi, C., Chen, L.: Geotrucrowd: trustworthy query answering with spatial crowdsourcing. In: International Conference on Advances in Geographic Information Systems, pp. 304–313. ACM (2013)
15. Deng, D., Shahabi, C., Demiryurek, U.: Maximizing the number of worker's self-selected tasks in spatial crowdsourcing. In: International Conference on Advances in Geographic Information Systems, pp. 324–333. ACM (2013)
16. Pournajaf, L., Xiong, L., Sunderam, V., et al. Spatial task assignment for crowd sensing with cloaked locations. In: International Conference on Mobile Data Management (MDM). IEEE (2014, to appear)
17. Rai, A., Chintalapudi, K.K., Padmanabhan, V.N., et al.: Zee: zero-effort crowdsourcing for indoor localization. In: International Conference on Mobile Computing and Networking. ACM, pp. 293–304 (2012)
18. Ghinita, G., Kalnis, P., Skiadopoulos, S.: MOBIHIDE: a mobilea peer-to-peer system for anonymous location-based queries. In: Papadias, D., Zhang, D., Kollios, G. (eds.) SSTD 2007. LNCS, vol. 4605, pp. 221–238. Springer, Heidelberg (2007)
19. Shokri, R., Theodorakopoulos, G., Le Boudec, J.Y., et al.: Quantifying location privacy. In: IEEE Symposium on International Conference on Security and Privacy (SP), pp. 247–262. IEEE (2011)
20. Shokri, R., Theodorakopoulos, G., Troncoso, C., et al.: Protecting location privacy: optimal strategy against localization attacks. In: International Conference on Computer and Communications Security (CCS), pp. 617–627. ACM (2012)
21. Narayanan, A., Thiagarajan, N., Lakhani, M., et al.: Location privacy via private proximity testing. In: International Conference on NDSS (2011)
22. Khoshgozaran, A., Shahabi, C., Shirani-Mehr, H.: Location privacy: going beyond K-anonymity, cloaking and anonymizers. Knowl. Inf. Syst. **26**(3), 435–465 (2011)
23. Guha, S., Jain, M., Padmanabhan, V.N.: Koi: a location-privacy platform for smartphone apps. In: International Conference on NSDI, pp. 183–196 (2012)
24. Cormode, G., Procopiuc, C., Srivastava, D., et al.: Differentially private spatial decompositions. In: IEEE 28th International Conference on Data Engineering (ICDE), pp. 20–31. IEEE (2012)
25. Kleinberg, J., Tardos, E.: Algorithm Design. Addison-Wesley Longman Publishing Co. Inc., Boston (2005)
26. Gowalla dataset. http://snap.stanford.edu/data/loc-gowalla.html
27. Cheng, P., Lian, X., Chen, Z., et al.: Reliable diversity-based spatial crowdsourcing by moving workers. arXiv preprint arXiv: 1412.0223 (2014)
28. Shahabi, C., et al.: Towards a generic framework for trustworthy spatial crowdsourcing. In: International Conference on Data Engineering for Wireless and Mobile Acess, pp. 1–4. ACM (2013)
29. Van Exel, M., Dias, E., Fruijtier, S.: The impact of crowdsourcing on spatial data quality indicators. In: Proceedings of GiScience 2011 (2010)

WDMA

A Trajectory Prediction Method for Location-Based Services

Huan Huo[1]([⊠]), Shang-ye Chen[2], Biao Xu[1], and Liang Liu[1]

[1] School of Optical-Electrical and Computer Engineering,
University of Shanghai for Science and Technology, Shanghai 200093, China
huo_huan@yahoo.com
[2] School of Information and Technology, Northwest University, Xi'an 710127, China

Abstract. Most existing location prediction techniques for moving objects on road network are mainly short-term prediction methods. In order to accurately predict the long-term trajectory, this paper first proposes a hierarchical road network model, to reduce the intersection vertexes of road network, which not only avoids unnecessary data storage and reduces complexity, but also improves the efficiency of the trajectory prediction algorithm. Based on this model, this paper proposes a detection backtracking algorithm, which deliberately selects the highest probability road fragment to improve the accuracy and efficiency of the prediction. Experiments show that this method is more efficient than other existing prediction methods.

1 Introduction

At present, most of the holistic trajectory prediction algorithms focus on free spaces solution [1,2], only few of them are based on moving objects in a real road network. And for those ones, they mostly just focus on the short-term predictions [3,4]. However, existing long-term prediction algorithms also fail to consider contextual information, which leads to a lot less accurate results especially at certain turning points.

To go beyond short-term prediction, this paper formulates a road network hierarchical model by analyzing a large number of historical trajectory data of moving objects. The model aims to reduce network complexity and capture the turning patterns at intersections. Based on the model, this paper presents a detection-backtracking algorithm to improve the accuracy and efficiency. It applies to both the short-term and long-term predictions even if the destination remains unknown, which also deals with dead ends and overlapping trajectories.

The rest of this paper is organized as follows. Section 2 discusses the related work. Section 3 formally introduces our prediction model. Section 4 introduces the prediction algorithm. Section 5 presents the experimental results of performance evaluation. Our conclusions are contained in Sect. 6.

© Springer International Publishing Switzerland 2015
R. Cai et al. (Eds.): APWeb 2015 Workshops, LNCS 9461, pp. 127–138, 2015.
DOI: 10.1007/978-3-319-28121-6_12

2   Preliminaries

The existing methods of location prediction for moving objects are roughly categorized to linear predictions [1,2] and non-linear predictions [3,5,6]. Usually, linear predictions are based on constant speeds and linear functions of time, while their variants may assume the constant speed at first but calculate the trajectories by factors such as edges or paths. And for those who combine edges with vectors [7], they surely perform well in predicting trajectories of moving objects with constant speeds in free spaces, but they might all readily break as they can't fit objects who are subject to real road networks which turn out to be much more perplexing.

Non-linear predictions use more complex mathematical equations than linear predictions do. Chen et al. [8] introduces SP method, which depends on Generalized Cellular Automata (GCA), using simulation and linear regression to predict the borders of future trajectories. Tao et al. [3] introduces a prediction model based on recursively-moving functions for those moving with uncertainty. Gaussian process regression model is also applied in trajectory predictions [5,6]. Those methods can only apply to non-linear movements instead of sudden turnings.

Karimi and Liu [9] introduce a Predictive Location Model (PLM), which applies a probability matrix to each intersection for calculating the probability of objects' turning each upcoming edge by analyzing their historical trajectories, and then uses a depth-wise algorithm to get new trajectories. However, Depth-wise search doesn't consider the probability of each turning, and the search range is based on the Euclidean Distance, namely, the object's current speed is multiplied by the time. That is might not accurate because the objects in real networks are always changing.

Kim et al. [10] comes up with a method that is similar to ours, but under their consideration, the destination is already known, while we assume it is not. Jeung et al. [11] introduces a PLM-based model as well as two prediction algorithms-Maximum Likelihood Algorithm (MLA) and Greedy Algorithm (GA). MLA is able to predict long trajectories, but once the duration is long enough to some level, it will need a lot more sub-trajectories to support its predictions, which drastically degrades the efficiency of the program. GA, in comparison, has a better performance on long-term predictions, but still, hasn't covered contextual information and leaves the problem of overlapping trajectories. Besides, it will be terminated as soon as a dead end comes up. A. Houenou et al. [4] combines CYRA with MRM, to predict vehicles' trajectories. The method tends to avoid collisions, but only in a very short period of time (namely, a few seconds), certainly not appealing to our interests of long-term predictions.

3   Prediction Model

In this section, we first define a hierarchical sketch on road network. Next we give some basic concepts and definitions for trajectory prediction based on the model. Then we describe our establishment of turning patterns at intersections.

3.1 Road Network Diagram and Sketch

Definition 1. Road Network Diagram

Road network diagram can be described as an undirected graph $G =< V, E >$, where V is the vertex set (the size is $|V|$) and E is the edge set (the size is $|E|$). Each vertex v ($v \in V$) represents an intersection, also a coordinate point $p = x, y$ in a two-dimensional space. Each edge $e = (v_i, v_j)$ ($v_i, v_j \in V, e \in E$) represents the edge between two intersections. Figure 1 illustrates the idea.

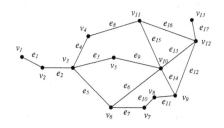

Fig. 1. Road network diagram   **Fig. 2.** Road network sketch

Definition 2. Vertex Degree and Connection Vertex

Given road network diagram $G =< V, E >$, $v_i \in V$, $deg(v_i)$ is equal to the number of edges connected to v_i. Vertex v_i is a connection vertex if $deg(v_i) \geq 2$.

Definition 3. Side Chain

Given a sequence of edges $S =< e_i, e_{i+1}, \cdots, e_{i+k} >$, S is a side chain if each vertex between two adjacent edges is a connection vertex.

Definition 4. Road Network Sketch

$G' =< V', E' >$ is the road network sketch, where V' is the vertex set after the removal of all the connection vertexes from V and E' is the edge set of side chains as well as those non-adjacent edges.

As shown in Fig. 1, the size of vertex set V ($|V|$) is 13 and that of edge set E ($|E|$) is 17. In Fig. 2, $|V'|$ is only 8 and $|E'|$ is 12. Note that by transferring G into G', we will be able to reduce the amount of vertexes and edges to simplify the whole model. The following discussions will all based on road network sketch. If not specified, We replace $G' =< V', E' >$ with $G =< V, E >$ for convenience.

3.2 Road Network Hierarchy

Given a large-scale network, trajectories of each moving object only cover relatively small part, leaving many roads and intersections unvisited. To further reduce the road network complexity and narrow down the search range, we adopt hierarchical strategy by observing the visit of an edge or an intersection.

Figure 2 contains 8 vertexes and 12 edges. Given E_v as the edge set of the visited trajectories, we divide the network into two layers-$G_1 =< V_1, E_1 >$ and $G_2 =< V_2, E_2 >$. Details about major steps of the process are as follows:

- *Step1.* Randomly select an $e_i =< v_i, v_j >$ ($e_i \in G$), where $deg(v_i) = 1$. If e_i is already in E_v, store (ei, vi, vj) into G_1. Otherwise, store them into G_2.
- *Step2.* Get the adjacent edge set of v_j as E_n. If E_n is not empty, iterate each edge $e_n =< v_j, v_k >\in E_n$. If $e_n \in E_v$, store (e_n, v_j, v_k) into G_1. Otherwise, store them into G_2. So far, if e_i is not in the same layer as e_n, connect corresponding vertex v_j in both G_1 and G_2 and establish a virtual edge ve_n.
- *Step3.* Repeat Step 2 until iterate all the vertexes in G, and formulate the hierarchical road network model.

Figure 3(a) shows part of a road network, where thick lines denote the historical trajectories. We first pick up $e_1 =< v_1, v_2 >$ as the starting edge. Since e_1 has been visited, we store (e_1, v_1, v_2) into G_1. Then we get $E_n = e_2, e_7$ as the adjacent edge set of v_2. As e_2 has been visited but e_7 has not, we store (e_2, v_2, v_3) and (e_7, v_2, v_6) into G_1 and G_2 respectively. Note that e_1 and e_7 are not in the same layer, so we establish a virtual edge ve_1 to connect the corresponding vertex v_2 in both G_1 and G_2. Similarly, e_3 and e_6 go to G_1, while e_4, e_5, e_8 and e_9 go to G_2. So we establish ve_2 and ve_3. Figure 3(b) shows the network model after hierarchy.

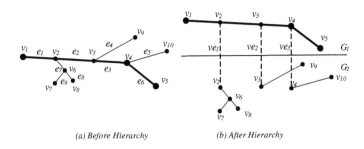

(a) Before Hierarchy   (b) After Hierarchy

Fig. 3. Example of hierarchical road network processing

3.3   Concepts and Definitions for Trajectory Predictions

Suppose $e = (v_i, v_j)$($e \in G$), then the position of a moving object on this edge can be expressed as $L = (e, d, p, t)$, with direction heading to vertex v_j, where e represents the current edge of the object, d is the distance between the object and v_i, p is the object's coordinate, t is the current time. The prediction duration T represents a time period as the object is moving from the current time t_c to a future time t_f. Given L and T, we can narrow down the trajectory prediction problem to analyzing the trajectory in $[t_c, t_{c+T}]$.

Definition 5. Trajectory
If we map each p to its corresponding position $L_i (i = 1, 2, 3 \cdots n)$, then a trajectory can be considered as an ascending time sequence with series of positions, which can be expressed as $Traj =< L_i, L_2 \cdots L_n >$.

Definition 6. Position Distance

Suppose L_i and L_j are two different positions of the same edge (both can be endpoints), then the distance between L_i and L_j is $Dist(L_i, L_j)$.

In order to evaluate the trajectory prediction query, consider two erroneous measurements: mean absolute error [12] and trajectory matching degree. As the position is described in two dimensional coordinate, we adopts L^2 norm.

Definition 7. Mean Absolute Error (MAE)

Suppose $\{L_{act1}, L_{act2}, \cdots, L_{actN}\}$ is the trajectory of a moving object in time period $[t_c, t_{c+T}]$, while $\{L_{pre1}, L_{pre2}, \cdots, L_{preN}\}$ is the predicted trajectory, we can calculate MAE as follows:

$$MAE = \frac{\sum_{i=1}^{N} |L_{prei} - L_{acti}|}{N} = \frac{\sum_{i=1}^{N} \left[(x_{prei} - x_{acti})^2 + (y_{prei} - y_{acti})^2 \right]^{1/2}}{N} \tag{1}$$

Definition 8. Trajectory Matching Degree (TMD)

Assume E_{act} is the actual trajectory edges set in between L_c and L_{act}, and E_{pre} is the predicted trajectory edges set in between L_c and L_{pre}, the precision and recall of the prediction can be described as $precision = \frac{|E_{act} \cap E_{pre}|}{|E_{pre}|}$ and $recall = \frac{|E_{act} \cap E_{pre}|}{|E_{act}|}$. Thus we adopts F1-score [13] as TMD:

$$F1 = \frac{2 \cdot precision \cdot recall}{precision + recall} \tag{2}$$

3.4 Turning Pattern at Intersections

The turning pattern problem of moving objects is the decisive factor to the prediction accuracy. In fact, many turning scenarios come with certainties, e.g., a car will make a specific turn when entering the highway and a man's daily drive usually follows a fixed route (home-company-home). We will take advantage of these information to find turning patterns for trajectory prediction.

Figure 4 shows part of a user's historical trajectories at an intersection. Each line represents a certain trajectory with an arrow pointing the direction and a label showing the class it belongs to. As during different time periods, the trajectories are different. Hence N number of time periods can divide trajectories into N classes, labeled as $0, 1, 2, ...N$. To simplify, we only use 1 and 0 as our class labels, which represents workday and weekend respectively.

Suppose the object has a state at every edge, when its current trajectory covers a new edge, we name it *state transition*. To illustrate state transition, we define O as the historical trajectory set, $Traj_o$ as the visited trajectory, e_{cur} as the current edge, e_i as the upcoming edge, c as the class label and E_v as the edge set connected to the vertex v.

So $Traj_o \to e_i$ is a *state transition*. If $Traj \to e_i$ is already covered in O and with a class c, we define $SP_o(Traj_o \to e_i)[c]$ as its *support degree*. So we give

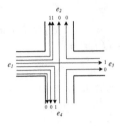

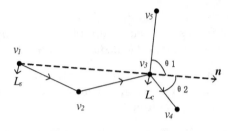

Fig. 4. Example of mobile object's historical trajectory at intersection

Fig. 5. Offset angle of road segment

the *state transition probability* (STP) of $Traj_o$ with a class c that is turning to e_i from v:

$$STP(v, Traj_o \rightarrow e_i)[c] = \frac{SP_o^\alpha(Traj_o \rightarrow e_i, c) \times \phi^\beta(e_i)}{\sum e_j \notin Traj_o SP_o^\alpha(Traj_o \rightarrow e_j, c) \times \phi^\beta(e_j)} \qquad (3)$$

We also define the STP of e_{cur}:

$$STP(v, e_{cur} \rightarrow e_i)[c] = \frac{SP_o^\alpha(e_{cur} \rightarrow e_i, c) \times \phi^\beta(e_i)}{\sum e_j \notin Traj_o SP_o^\alpha(e_{cur} \rightarrow e_j, c) \times \phi^\beta(e_j)} \qquad (4)$$

$\phi(e_i)$ in Eqs. 3 and 4 represents offset factor on e_i, which is usually considered to be the reciprocal of offset angle θ_i (see Eq. 6). For a moving object, the smaller θ_i it has, the bigger $\phi(e_i)$ it gets, so is STP. α and β are the support degree and offset factor weight, respectively.

According to Eqs. 3 and 4, we can predict the next edge e_{next} that the object is about to turn:

$$e_{next} = \begin{cases} arg_{e_i} max(STP(v_{cur}, Traj_o \rightarrow e_i)[c]) & \text{if } Traj_o \rightarrow e_i exist \\ arg_{e_i} max(STP(v_{cur}, e_{cur} \rightarrow e_i)[c]) & else \end{cases} \qquad (5)$$

In the lack of historical trajectories, driving directions become the decisive factor to predict e_{next}. As shown in Fig. 5, θ is the offset angle between direction vector n and edge vector e, L_c is the initial position of a moving object, L_s is the intersection the object currently in, E_a is the set of unvisited edges connected to the vertex, we choose the edge as our e_{next} with the smallest θ by using cosine formula:

$$e_{next} = arg_{e_i \in E_a} min(\theta_{e_i}) = \begin{cases} \theta_i \in (0°, 180°) \\ n = (x_c - x_s, y_c - y_s) \\ e_i = (x_i - x_c, y_i - y_c) \\ arg_{e_i \in E_a} max(cos\theta_{e_i}) = arg_{e_i \in E_a} max(\frac{n \cdot e_i}{|n| \cdot |e_i|}) \end{cases} \qquad (6)$$

4 Prediction Algorithm

4.1 Algorithm Design

This paper presents a *detection backtracking algorithm* (DBT). Algorithm 1 searches the edge with maximum STP and Algorithm 2 is the detailed pseudo code of DBT.

Algorithm 1. maxSTP(*state, c, v, V, G, α, β*)

Input: state *state*, class *c*, current vertex *v*, set of vertexes visited *V*, road network diagram *G*, *α* and *β* are the support degree and the offset factor weight, respectively.
Output: the edge with maximum STP
1: total=[]; theta=[]; states={}
2: **for** edge in *G* **do**
3:     get all state transition trajectory of class *c* at vertex *v*, and save to states, their value is initialized to 0
4: **end for**
5: **for** trajectory in *G* **do**
6:     **for** state in states **do**
7:         calculate the total number of every state trajectory of class *c* and their offset angle(see Eq. 6), and save them to total and theta respectively
8:     **end for**
9:     **if** every value is empty in total **then**
10:         **return** 0
11:     **end if**
12: **end for**
13: **for** state in states **do**
14:     calculate state transition probability of each state by the Eq. 3 and Eq. 4, and covering saved to states
15: **end for**
16: sort(state)

In reality, a single factor sometimes can lead to a very complex prediction model, so most existing algorithms exclude the factors we mentioned in Sect. 1 (e.g. contextual information, loop and etc.). We list four cases below:

- Arrest point. Moving objects are not moving all the time. For example, in situations like buying coffee when heading off to work or going shopping on the way home, it usually takes several minutes or hours to stay at a certain spot, which referred as arrest point. Given the current trajectory's class, by analyzing historical trajectories and calculating the gathering numbers of spots, we are able to tell which case the arrest point belongs to.
- Loop. In most cases, it is not possible to form a loop, because moving objects usually head toward their designated places, which is closely related to human behaviors. However, there are some exceptions. For example, a driver has to go home for some important documents even though he or she is half way to work. But these are small probability events, so we leave them out.

Algorithm 2. DBT(G, L, λ_{stop}, T)

Input: road network diagram after hierarchy G, moving object's current position $L = (e, d, p, t)$, time threshold of arrest points λ_{stop}, class c, prediction duration T

Output: Trajectory $Traj$

1: e_{cur}=L['e']
2: v_{cur} = mobile object being approach to end vertex of e_{cur}
3: $t = \text{Dist}(L, v_{cur})/\text{Speed}(e_{cur})$
4: $E_{visted} = []$; $V_{visited} = []$; $Traj = []$
5: **while** $t < T$ **do**
5:     $V_{visited}$.append(v_{cur}); $E_{visited}$.apppend(e_{cur})
5:     $Traj$.append((e_{cur}, Dist(L,v_{cur}) , v_{cur}.get(p), v_{cur}.get(t)))
6:     **if** deg(v_{cur})==1 **then**
7:         **if** e_{cur}==L. get(e) **then**
8:             return $Traj$.append('e':e_{cur}, 'd':Dist(e_{cur},e_{before})-L.get(d), 't':p,T)
9:         **else**
10:            backtrack to previous vertex and go on
11:        **end if**
12:    **else**
13:        e_{next}=maxSTP($Traj$, c, v_{cur}, $V_{visited}$, G, α, β)
14:        **if** not e_{next} **then**
15:            e_{next}=the offset angle of edge is smallset
16:            **if** not e_{next} **then**
17:                popEdge = $Traj$.pop()
18:                V_{state}.append(v_{cur})
19:                backtrack to previous vertex and go on
20:            **end if**
21:        **end if**
22:    **end if**
23: **end while**
24: v_{before}=v_{cur}; e_{before}=e_{cur}
25: v_{cur} = another vertex of e_{next}, don't visited
26: e_{cur}=e_{next}
27: t=t+Dist(v_{before},v_{cur}) / Speed(e_{cur})
28: **if** abs(Dist(p, v_{before})/Speed(e_{cur}))-time)$\geq\lambda_{stop}$ **then**
29:     v_{cur}=v_{before}; e_{cur}=e_{before}
30: **end if**
31: $Traj$.append((e_{cur}, Dist(L,v_{cur}), v_{cur}.get(p), v_{cur}.get(t)))
32: **return** $Traj$

- Partially overlapping trajectories will lead to turning errors. In Fig. 6, if we use probability matrix [9] and mobile transferring probabilistic method [11], $e_2 \rightarrow e_4 \rightarrow e_6$ will increase the probability of turning e_6 at intersection v_2 to $2/3$, the predicted trajectory will be $e_1 \rightarrow e_4 \rightarrow e_6$, which is obviously wrong. As the trajectories partially overlapped in some edges might lead to wrong trajectory, we gave e_{next} in Eq. 5 at first to avoid the problem.
- No historical trajectory exists. Refer to Eq. 6, it will help to pick the right edge to turn to by calculating deviation angle θ of a moving object.

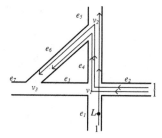

Fig. 6. Overlapping road segment of trajectory

4.2 Time Complexity Analysis

Suppose the number of traversed vertexes during one prediction is $|V'|$, then $O(|V'|)$ is the time complexity for one traversal. But we also have to calculate the highest STP at each vertex and query the historical time spent on the current edge. In this paper, we use binary search algorithm, the time complexity is $O(2 \cdot log|V|)$. Together, the total time complexity of our algorithm is $O(2 \cdot |V'| \cdot log|V|)$. In fact, we only count $O(log|V|)$ because $|V'|$ can be taken as a constant since our algorithm usually only traverse a few vertexes. As k increases, it needs more time to do pruning, also has to compute more MBRs, leading to the increasing time consumption of the algorithm.

5   Experimental Evaluation

We compare our algorithm with OLM [9] and Greedy [11] on calculating MAE and F1-score. The data set used covers trajectories of 182 individuals in 5 years of Beijing traffic, with total 18,670 trajectories and 24,876,978 positions. And our road network data consist of 433,391 edges and 171,504 intersections.

Since all the trajectories are GPS records, the presence of sampling error is inevitable. Besides, the trajectories in experiment need to be generated from real road network. Therefore, we preprocess the data set by analyzing the trajectory similarity [14] and using trajectory interpolation and map-matching [15]. In the paper, we use simple linear interpolation [16] and ST-Matching algorithm [17], more specifically in [14,16,17].

We randomly select $1,000$ processed trajectories as the test set. α and β are set to 4 and 1, respectively. For each trajectory, we choose an initial position, then predict under different prediction duration (increments by 5 min).

Figure 7 compares different methods by MAE under different predicted duration with total 2000 trajectories, where MAE values of DBT are about 2km and 14km lower than those of Greedy and PLM on average. In Fig. 7, DBT algorithm is more accurate in predicting destinations than the other two methods.

We also consider the F1-score in Fig. 8. By comparison, even though the F1-score of DBT is falling with the rising predicted time, it still maintains a

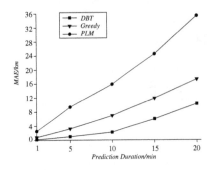 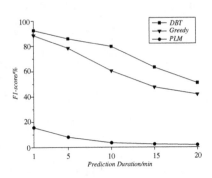

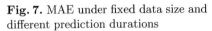

Fig. 7. MAE under fixed data size and different prediction durations

Fig. 8. F1-score under fixed data size and different prediction durations

relatively high and stable performance better than Greedy algorithm, while PLM turns out to be the worst.

By observing Figs. 7 and 8, we can conclude that DBT performs better in shorter period of time, namely, 10 min. This is because when running into an intersection, DBT only calculates the STP of $Traj_o$, not the STP of e_{cur}, avoiding the presence of turning errors caused by overlapping trajectories. Note that PLM performs very bad in both cases, because the calculating errors of finding the exit point tend to be pretty large in PLM. Also seen from Figs. 9 and 10, as data scale grows, MAE becomes lower, but F1-score gets higher, which means more information can be obtained to improve our predictions.

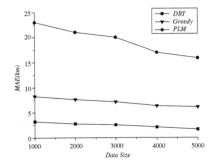 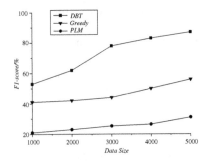

Fig. 9. MAE under fixed prediction duration and different data sizes

Fig. 10. F1-score under fixed prediction duration and different data sizes

Next, we compare our algorithm performance by analyzing the average computation time. We use Python to implement the algorithms. All experiments are run on a PC with 2.60 GHz CPU and 4 GB of main memory. As shown in Fig. 11, DBT maintains its high performance due to the road network hierarchy. Greedy also has a good performance, but not as well as DBT, since it doesn't

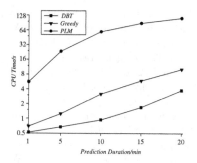 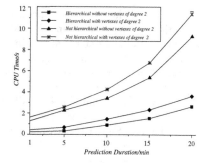

Fig. 11. CPU processing time under different prediction durations

Fig. 12. CPU processing time under different circumstances

consider contextual information at all. Meanwhile, as PLM always has to traverse all the trajectories from current position to find the exit point, when the length of prediction increases, PLM's efficiency will significantly decrease.

We compare the CPU processing time under different circumstances in Fig. 12. The results are pretty clear that both the hierarchy of road network and the removal of vertexes with degree 2 have discernible effects on efficiency improvement, especially the hierarchy.

6 Conclusion

This paper presents a hierarchical road network model to reduce complexity and improve the efficiency of prediction algorithm. We propose BDT to deal with contextual information and trajectories' overlapping problems that most existing algorithms haven't covered yet. Our experiments show that BDT is more accurate with high performance in both short-term and long-term predictions. Our future work will take more context information [18] into account to further improve the accuracy.

Acknowledgment. This work is supported by National Natural Science Foundation of China (61003031, 61202376), Shanghai Engineering Research Center Project (*GCZX14014*), Shanghai Key Science and Technology Project in IT(14511107902), Shanghai Leading Academic Discipline Project(*XTKX2012*) and Hujiang Research Center Special Foundation(*C*14001)

References

1. Jensen, C.S., Lin, D., Ooi, B.C.: Query and update efficient b+-tree based indexing of moving objects. In: Proceedings of the Thirtieth International Conference on Very Large Data Bases-Volume 30. VLDB Endowment, pp. 768–779 (2004)
2. Jensen, C.S., Lin, D., Ooi, B.C., Zhang, R..: Effective density queries on continuouslymoving objects. In: Proceedings of the 22nd International Conference on Data Engineering ICDE 2006, pp. 71–71. IEEE (2006)

3. Tao, Y., Faloutsos, C., Papadias, D., Liu, B.: Prediction and indexing of moving objects with unknown motion patterns. In: Proceedings of the 2004 ACM SIGMOD International Conference on Management of Data, pp. 611–622. ACM (2004)

4. Houenou, A., Bonnifait, P., Cherfaoui, V., Yao, W.: Vehicle trajectory prediction based on motion model and maneuver recognition. In 2013 IEEE/RSJ International Conference on Intelligent Robots and Systems, pp. 4363–4369. IEEE (2013)

5. Heravi, E.J., Khanmohammadi, S.: Long term trajectory prediction of moving objects using gaussian process. In: 2011 First International Conference on Robot, Vision and Signal Processing (RVSP), pp. 228–232. IEEE (2011)

6. Ellis, D., Sommerlade, E., Reid, I..: Modelling pedestrian trajectory patterns with gaussian processes. In: 12th International Conference on Computer Vision Workshops (ICCV Workshops), pp. 1229–1234. IEEE (2009)

7. Jensen, C.S., Pakalnis, S.: Trax: real-world tracking of moving objects. In: Proceedings of the 33rd International Conference on Very Large Data Bases. VLDB Endowment, pp. 1362–1365 (2007)

8. Chen, J., Meng, X.: Moving Objects Management. Trajectory Prediction of Moving Objects, pp. 105–112. Springer, Heidelberg (2010)

9. Karimi, H.A., Liu, X.: A predictive location model for location-based services. In: Proceedings of the 11th ACM International Symposium on Advances in Geographic Information Systems, pp. 126–133. ACM (2003)

10. Kim, S.-W., Won, J.-I., Kim, J.-D., Shin, M., Lee, J.-H., Kim, H.: Path prediction of moving objects on road networks through analyzing past trajectories. In: Apolloni, B., Howlett, R.J., Jain, L. (eds.) KES 2007, Part I. LNCS (LNAI), vol. 4692, pp. 379–389. Springer, Heidelberg (2007)

11. Jeung, H., Yiu, M.L., Zhou, X., Jensen, C.S.: Path prediction and predictive range querying in road network databases. VLDB J. **19**(4), 585–602 (2010)

12. Zuo, Y., Liu, G., Yue, X., Wang, W., Wu, H.: Similarity matching over uncertain time series. In: Seventh International Conference on Computational Intelligence and Security (CIS) 2011. IEEE, pp. 1357–1361 (2011)

13. Baeza-Yates, R., Ribeiro-Neto, B., et al.: Modern Information Retrieval. ACM press, New York (1999)

14. Guohua, L., Wu Honghua, W.W.: Similarity matching for uncertain time series. J. Comput. Res. Dev. **51**(8), 585–602 (2014)

15. Guo, C., Liu, J.N., Fang, Y., Luo, M., Cui, J.S.: Value extraction and collaborative mining methods for location big data. Ruan Jian Xue Bao/J. Softw. **25**(4), 713–730 (2014)

16. Liu, S., Liu, Y., Ni, L.M., Fan, J., Li, M.: Towards mobility-based clustering. In: Proceedings of the 16th ACM SIGKDD International Conference on Knowledge Discovery and Data Mining, pp. 919–928. ACM (2010)

17. Lou, Y., Zhang, C., Zheng, Y., Xie, X., Wang, W., Huang, Y.: Map-matching for low-sampling-rate gps trajectories. In: 17th ACM SIGSPATIAL International Conference on Advances in Geographic Information Systems, pp. 352–361. ACM (2009)

18. Gu, H., Gartrell, M., Zhang, L., Lv, Q., Grunwald, D.: Anchormf: towards effective event context identification. In: 22nd ACM International Conference on Information and Knowledge Management. CIKM, pp. 629–638 (2013)

Cross-Lingual Entity Query from Large-Scale Knowledge Graphs

Yonghao Su, Chi Zhang, Jinyang Li, Chengyu Wang, Weining Qian[✉],
and Aoying Zhou

Institute for Data Science and Engineering, ECNU-PINGAN Innovative Research
Center for Big Data, East China Normal University, Shanghai, China
{suyonghao,chizhang,jinyangli,chengyuwang}@ecnu.cn,
{wnqian,ayzhou}@sei.ecnu.edu.cn

Abstract. A knowledge graph is a structured knowledge system which contains a huge amount of entities and relations. It plays an important role in the field of named entity query. DBpedia, YAGO and other English knowledge graphs provide open access to huge amounts of high-quality named entities. However, Chinese knowledge graphs are still in the development stage, and contain fewer entities. The relations between entities are not rich. A natural question is: how to use mature English knowledge graphs to query Chinese named entities, and to obtain rich relation networks. In this paper, we propose a Chinese entity query system based on English knowledge graphs. For entities we build up links between Chinese entities and English knowledge graphs. The basic idea is to build a cross-lingual entity linking model, RSVM, between Chinese and English Wikipedia. RSVM is used to build cross-lingual links between Chinese entities and English knowledge graphs. The experiments show that our approach can achieve a high precision of 82.3 % for the task of finding cross-lingual entities on a test dataset. Our experiments for the sub task of finding missing cross-lingual links show that our approach has a precision of 89.42 % with a recall of 80.47 %.

Keywords: Cross-lingual entity linking · Knowledge graph · Entity disambiguation · Semantic query

1 Introduction

Over the past years, the amount of knowledge grows rapidly, but stored in an unstructured way. Knowledge graphs can describe entities structurally, and we can get attributes about entities. For example, when we query entity "图灵",, *Turing* in English, in a Chinese knowledge graph, we may get some information about *Turing*, such as *Turing* was male and came from the UK. But we want to know more about *Turing*, such as which university he graduated from. However, Chinese knowledge graphs contain fewer entities and relations between entities are not rich [14]. We can not fully describe the entity *Turing* in Chinese. English knowledge graphs contain rich entities and relations, which can describe

© Springer International Publishing Switzerland 2015
R. Cai et al. (Eds.): APWeb 2015 Workshops, LNCS 9461, pp. 139–150, 2015.
DOI: 10.1007/978-3-319-28121-6_13

entities comprehensively [3,9,10,18]. But the cross-lingual links between English knowledge graphs and Chinese knowledge graphs are rare. It will lead to a low recall to use English knowledge graph directly. Typically, the cross-lingual links are manually added by authors of articles and are incomplete or erroneous. When the author of an article does not link to an article which expresses to the same concept in an other language version of Wikipedia. This is called a *missing cross-lingual link*.

It is vital to find such entity in English knowledge graphs with the same meaning of the Chinese query entity. It needs to solve two problems: (a) entity disambiguation and (b) cross-lingual entity linking. The challenge (a) has already been addressed by other researchers [4,5,7,11]. A group of highly related works for challenge (b) has been proposed by [1,6,12,15,16]. But these algorithms do not fit our query task. The methods of entity disambiguation are based on the same language version of Wikipedia, but we need solve the entity disambiguation task in two different versions of Wikipedia. Moreover, the cross-lingual algorithms can not deal with the structure challenge in Wikipedia as shown in Fig. 2. The problem of query Chinese entities in English knowledge graphs is non-trivial and challenging, summarized as follows:

Cross-Lingual Entity Disambiguation. We treat cross-lingual entity disambiguation task as two sub tasks: entity disambiguation and re-ranking candidate entities disambiguated in other language version of knowledge graphs. Existing methods for entity disambiguation are for the same language. They can not be used for cross-lingual entity disambiguation directly. We propose a method that use a vector space model to solve entity disambiguation problem, and get a set of candidates. With the help of our cross-lingual entity linking module, we re-rank the candidates to achieve cross-lingual entity disambiguation.

Cross-Lingual Entity Linking. A large amount of new knowledge is frequently added in Chinese knowledge graphs or English knowledge graphs. The structures of these new knowledge graphs are sparse. But exiting methods heavily depend on structure features, thus we must find other unstructured features to describe the relations between cross-lingual entities.

In this paper, we propose a cross-lingual entity query system CLEQS based on Chinese Wikipedia, English Wikipedia and links between them. The novelties of CLEQS as shown below: (a) We can find missing entity links between Chinese knowledge graphs and English knowledge graphs. (b) In entity disambiguation task we obtain a set of candidates instead of only one candidate and (c) we design a method to re-rank the candidates with the help of structure relations in YAGO [9], which contains 1 million entities and 5 million facts, as the English data source. In this way, we get high precision in the cross-lingual query task, especially in the entity disambiguation task. (d) Because the structure features are less important when more and more entities are added into Wikipedia as shown in Fig. 2, we pay more attention to semantic features and design a set of semantic features to improve query accuracy.

More precisely, given a Chinese entity mention and its context, CLEQS uses a vector space model in order to effectively identify a set of candidate entities in Chinese Wikipedia. For each candidate entity in the resulting candidate set, a *ranking SVM* model with a set of structure and semantic features are used to find the cross-lingual links in YAGO, and finally we use structure features in YAGO to re-rank the candidate result sets. We evaluate CLEQS and the two sub tasks of CLEQS on a dataset of 1000 pairs of articles. The result that we obtain show that CLEQS performs very well.

The remainder of the paper is organized as follows. Section 2 outlines some related work. Section 3 formally defines the problem of knowledge linking and some related concepts. Section 4 describes the proposed cross-lingual query approach. Section 5 presents the evaluation results and finally Sect. 6 concludes this work.

2 Related Work

The problem of entity disambiguation has been addressed by many researchers starting from Bagga and Baldwin [4], who use the bag of words and vector cosine similarity to represent the context of the entity mention. Jiang et al. [7] adopt the graph based framework to extend the similarity metric to disambiguate the entity mentions effectively. Researchers have shown a great interest in mapping textual entity mention to its corresponding entity in the knowledge base. Bunescu and Pasca [5] firstly deal with this problem by extracting a set of features derived from Wikipedia for entity detection and disambiguation. They use the bag of words and cosine similarity to measure the relation between the context of the mention and the text of the Wikipedia articles. Shen et al. [11] present a framework named LINDEN, and propose a set of semantic features to disambiguate English entities based on YAGO.

The problem of missing cross-lingual links has attracted increasing attention. A group of highly related work has been proposed based on Wikipedia. ADaFre and Rijke [1] exploit the structure features between Wikipedia to find missing entity links. Wentland et al. [16] extract multilingual contexts for named entities contained in Wikipedia by considering the cross-lingual link structure of Wikipedia. Sorg and Cimiano [12] propose a method, which uses SVM model [6] with structure features, to find missing cross-lingual links between English and German Wikipedia. Wang et al. [15] discover missing cross-lingual links between Chinese Wikipedia and English Wikipedia by using factor graph model.

3 Problem Formulation

In this section, we formally define the cross-lingual query problem. This problem can be decomposed into two sub problems: cross-lingual entity linking and cross-lingual entity disambiguation. Here, we first define the *entity query* and *entity disambiguation* as follows.

Definition 1. Entity query. *Given a knowledge graph K, unstructured text T, entity p in K and entity e in T. If K contains entity p, which can uniquely map to e, we call this process entity query. When the knowledge graph K and unstructured text T are in different languages, we call it cross-lingual entity query.*

Definition 2. Entity disambiguation. *Given a knowledge graph K and named entity sets $E = \{e_1, e_2, ..., e_n\}$ in which elements have the same surface form. If we can find elements in K mapping to E for each element e_i. We call this process entity disambiguation. When the knowledge graph K and named entity sets E are in different languages, we call it cross-lingual entity disambiguation.*

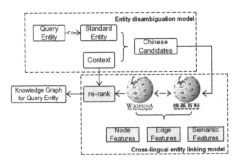

Fig. 1. The framework of the system

We first use existing cross-lingual links in Wikipedia to find out the important factors of knowledge linking, which is the core module in cross-lingual entity query. Here, we download English Wikipedia and Chinese Wikipedia dumps from Wikipedia's website and extract cross-lingual links between them. We extract 450 thousand cross-lingual links (KCL) between Chinese and English Wikipedia. The Chinese version of Wikipedia is considered as a directed graph W_{zh}, The English Wikipedia is considered as W_{en}, where each node n_α represents a Wikipedia article in the language version α of Wikipedia, and has inlinks $in(n_\alpha)$, outlinks $out(n_\alpha)$ and categories $cat(n_\alpha)$.

We first investigate how important structure features are in cross-lingual links prediction. If two articles, n_{zh}, n_{en}, link to two other equivalent articles, we say the two articles have a *common outlink* $col(n_{zh}, n_{en})$. Similarly, if n_{zh}, n_{en} are linked by two other equivalent articles, we say they have a *common inlink* $cil(n_{zh}, n_{en})$. The *common categories* of n_{zh}, n_{en} are called $ccl(n_{zh}, n_{en})$. Because YAGO uses WordNet as its taxonomy instead of Wikipedia category. We only calculate the probabilities of being equivalent conditioned on the number of $col(n_{zh}, n_{en})$ and $cil(n_{zh}, n_{en})$ between n_{zh} in YAGO and n_{en} in English Wikipedia. The number of $col(n_{zh}, n_{en})$ accounts for 85.94 % of total links in YAGO, and the number of $cil(n_{zh}, n_{en})$ is 92.88 %. It is obvious that we can exploit relations between YAGO and Wikipedia to sort the candidate YAGO entities.

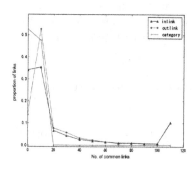

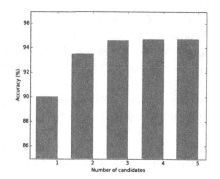

Fig. 2. Distribution of common links between Chinese Wiki. and English Wiki.

Fig. 3. The cumulative distribution of query entity being found

Due to the fact that more entities are added into Wikipedia, we find that structure features have a smaller effect on cross-lingual entity linking problem. We evaluate the number of $col(n_{zh}, n_{en})$, $cil(n_{zh}, n_{en})$ and $ccl(n_{zh}, n_{en})$ in set KCL. It is obvious that structure features are less important, as shown in Fig. 2.

Figure 1 shows the framework of our system. Where standard entity is the name of the surface form of Chinese query entity m, and context is the bag of words around entity m. We consider two aspects: accurate structure entity links and accurate entity disambiguation. To solve the two problem, we construct entity disambiguation module and cross-lingual entity linking module. The detail description of each module is shown in Sects. 4.1 and 4.2.

In this paper, entity disambiguation is defined as the task to map a textual named entity m, which is already recognized in the unstructured text, to a unique entity e in Wikipedia. We use the bag of words model to represent the context of the entity mention, and obtain the candidate entities in YAGO based on the vector cosine similarity. Cross-lingual entity linking module interacts between Chinese Wikipedia and English Wikipedia. This module finds the English entity describing the same concept of Chinese entity, and finds the missing cross-lingual entity links between Chinese Wikipedia and English Wikipedia. We treat cross-lingual entity linking as a ranking problem, and use Ranking SVM with a set of semantic features and structure features to find cross-lingual entity links.

4 The Proposed Approach

In this section, we describe our proposed method and two modules in detail.

4.1 Entity Disambiguation

Candidate Entity Generation. Given an entity m, the set of candidate entities E_m should have the name of the surface form of m. To solve this problem, we need to build a dictionary that contains vast amount of information about the surface forms of entities, like abbreviations and nicknames, etc. We use Wikipedia, which contains a set of useful features for the construction of the dictionary we need. We use the following three structures of Wikipedia to build the dictionary about the surface forms of entities:

Entity pages: Each entity page in Wikipedia describes a unique entity and the information focusing on this entity.

Redirect pages: A redirect page maps an alternative name to the page of formal name, such as synonym terms and abbreviations in Wikipedia.

Disambiguation pages: A disambiguation page is created to explain and link to entity pages, which is given the same name in Wikipedia.

Candidate Entity Disambiguation. The named entities express different concepts in different contexts. For example, entity "Michael Jordan" refers to the famous NBA player or the Berkeley professor in different contexts. In this paper, we use vector space model to represent the contexts of the entity mention and use the vector cosine similarity to calculate the similarity between the contexts of query entity and article in Wikipedia. The stop-words in the contexts of query entity lead to a higher vector dimension and make words feature unobvious. Thus, we use TF-IDF [2] to filter out the stop words.

4.2   Cross-Lingual Entity Linking

In this paper, we treat cross-lingual entity linking as a ranking problem, we construct a Ranking SVM with a set of structure features and semantic features between Chinese Wikipedia and English Wikipedia. Ranking SVM is an ranking model using machine learning algorithm, which is proposed by Joachims [8]. The optimization objective of Ranking SVM is to minimize the objective function. Interested readers please refer to [8] for details:

$$Min : V(\overrightarrow{w}, \overrightarrow{\xi}) = \frac{1}{2}\overrightarrow{w}^T \cdot \overrightarrow{w} + C\sum \xi_{i,j,k} \tag{1}$$

Subject to:

$$\overrightarrow{w}\Phi(q_1, di) > \overrightarrow{w}\Phi(q_1, dj) + 1 - \xi_{i,j,1}$$
$$...$$
$$\overrightarrow{w}\Phi(q_n, di) > \overrightarrow{w}\Phi(q_n, dj) + 1 - \xi_{i,j,n} \tag{2}$$

$$\forall i \forall j \forall k : \xi_{i,j,k} > 0 \tag{3}$$

where C is a margin size against training error and $\xi_{i,j,k}$ is a parameter of slack variables.

Feature Design. From the observation of Fig. 2, we know the structure features are less important in cross-lingual entity links. Because if one cross-lingual entity link pair describes the same concept, the contents of them are similar with each other. So we design a set of semantic features and some structure features. In the following part, we introduce the definition of structure features and semantic features in detail.

Structure Features. We treat Chinese Wikipedia combining with English Wikipedia as a graph. In the graph, we view articles as nodes, common inlink, common outlink and links to categories as edges.

Common rate feature. (a) We design features for inlinks, outlinks and categories. We use the rate between common links and all links between Chinese Wikipeida entity and English Wikipedia entity formally:

$$\forall n_\alpha \in W_{zh}, \exists n_\beta \in W_{en}, if\ \exists col(n_\alpha, n_\beta)\ then\ n_\beta \in CI^\beta(n_\alpha)$$
$$\forall n_\alpha \in W_{zh}, \exists n_\beta \in W_{en}, if\ \exists cil(n_\alpha, n_\beta)\ then\ n_\beta \in CO^\beta(n_\alpha)$$
$$\forall n_\alpha \in W_{zh}, \exists n_\beta \in W_{en}, if\ \exists ccl(n_\alpha, n_\beta)\ then\ n_\beta \in CC^\beta(n_\alpha)$$

We define f_{in}, f_{out} and f_{cat} to describe *common rate features*:

$$f_{in} = \frac{|\ CI^{en}(n_{zh})\ |}{|\ in_{zh}\ | + |\ in_{en}\ |}$$
$$f_{out} = \frac{|\ CO^{en}(n_{zh})\ |}{|\ out_{zh}\ | + |\ out_{en}\ |} \qquad (4)$$
$$f_{cat} = \frac{|\ CC^{en}(n_{zh})\ |}{|\ cat_{zh}\ | + |\ cat_{en}\ |}$$

(b) As shown in Fig. 2, every intervals have their own rates for links. We classify links into 10 intervals according to the rate in Fig. 2.

Coherence feature. We have extracted 450 thousand known cross-lingual links between Chinese Wikipedia and English Wikipedia. We calculate the coherence between common links and their links in known cross-lingual links.

$$\forall n_\alpha \in W_\alpha, \exists col(n_\alpha, n_\beta) \in KCL\ and\ n_\beta \in W_\beta,\ then\ n_\beta \in KCO^\beta(n_\alpha)$$
$$\forall n_\alpha \in W_\alpha, \exists cil(n_\alpha, n_\beta) \in KCL\ and\ n_\beta \in W_\beta,\ then\ n_\beta \in KCI^\beta(n_\alpha)$$
$$\forall n_\alpha \in W_\alpha, \exists ccl(n_\alpha, n_\beta) \in KCL\ and\ n_\beta \in W_\beta,\ then\ n_\beta \in KCC^\beta(n_\alpha)$$

We define fc_{in}, fc_{out} and fc_{cat} to describe *coherence features*:

$$fc_{in} = \frac{|\ CI^{en}(n_{zh})\ |}{|\ KCI^{en}(n_{zh})\ | + |\ KCI^{zh}(n_{en})\ |}$$
$$fc_{out} = \frac{|\ CO^{en}(n_{zh})\ |}{|\ KCO^{en}(n_{zh})\ | + |\ KCO^{zh}(n_{en})\ |} \qquad (5)$$
$$fc_{cat} = \frac{|\ CC^{en}(n_{zh})\ |}{|\ KCC^{en}(n_{zh})\ | + |\ KCC^{zh}(n_{en})\ |}$$

Semantic Features. The articles of Chinese Wikipedia and English Wikipedia are similar with each other in semantics if they describe the same entity. Articles consist of abstract, main body of text and relevant titles of articles in Wikipedia. Every word in one article has its own POS tag, we assume that noun term is the most important part of one article. One problem is that a Chinese noun can be mapped to a set of English noun. To solve this problem, we translate Chinese noun to English noun with the help of Chinese-English Dictionary and WordNet [10]. We find the English translation for the Chinese noun, then we get the Synset the English noun is seated. We use all the words in this Synset as the result. We create three features based on brief introduction, full text and relevant Wikipedia entities.

Abstract similarity feature. We calculate the similarity of the abstract between Chinese Wikipedia article and English Wikipedia article by calculating the count of noun similarity.

Full text similarity feature. We calculate the similarity of full text between Chinese Wikipedia and English Wikipedia.

Entity coherence similarity feature. We caluculate the full text similarity of the entities in the context of Chinese Wikipeida article and English Wikipedia article.

4.3   Cross-Lingual Disambiguation Accuracy Improving

Through the above process, we get some candidate entities in YAGO. Then we re-rank this candidate entities by the relevant entities linked with the candidate entity. We calculate the Semantic Associativity [17] use Eq. (6) between Chinese entity mention and candidate entities in YAGO.

$$SimSA(e_1, e_2) = 1 - \frac{log(max(|E_1|, |E_2|)) - log(|E_1 \cap E_2|)}{log(|W|) - log(min(|E_1|, |E_2|))} \tag{6}$$

where e_1 is the English entity which has the same means with Chinese entity. e_2 is the English entity which has the same means with candidate entities in YAGO. E_1 and E_2 are the sets of English Wikipedia entities that link to e_1 and e_2, and W is the set of all entities in English Wikipedia.

5   Expriments

5.1   Datasets

In order to evaluate our approach, we construct two datasets for entity disambiguation task and cross-lingual entity linking task.

EDD. In order to evaluate our approach, we construct a dataset named EDD that contains article pairs from Baidu Baike (a large scale Chinese Wiki knowledge base) and Chinese Wikipedia. We randomly select 1000 article pairs from the dataset to test entity disambiguation module. Each article pair contains a

Baike article and a Wikipedia article, both of which express the same concept. The knowledge graph we adopt in this work is YAGO [9]. The reason why we choose YAGO as the knowledge graph is that YAGO contains more than 1 millon entities and 5 millon facts, and we can use the rich facts to describe one entity comprehensively.

CLD. In cross-lingual entity linking module, we construct a dataset named CLD that contains article pairs form Chinese Wikipedia and English Wikipedia. we selected 1000 English articles with cross-lingual links to Chinese articles from Wikipedia. We generate all possible 1000 × 1000 article pairs from selected articles. 1000 of them in English-Chinese article pairs linked by cross-lingual links are labeled as positive examples and the rest of articles are negative examples. If we choose this training data, the negative pairs are far more than positive. It will cause the problem of overlap. From Fig. 2, we find about 92 % English-Chinese article pairs have common outlinks in KCL. So we restrict the number of inequivalent pairs by common outlinks. After restriction, we control the ratio between positive and negative to be 1:5.

EDD and CLD have the same set of Chinese Wikipedia articles. We can evaluate entity disambiguation task and cross-lingual entity linking task together.

5.2   Performance Evaluation

Evaluation of Entity Disambiguation. The entity disambiguation is a crucial step for CLEQS because it can affect the input of the cross-lingual entity linking module. In particular, we have marked the named entities in unstructured text. The evaluation of this module is to compare the precision. we use EDD to obtain the best number of the candidate entities in Chinese Wikipedia. In Fig. 3 we show the histogram of the accuracy that real entity in these candidates with the grow of the candidate number.

The accuracy in Fig. 3 shows that with the increase of the candidate number, the accuracy of finding article in Chinese Wikipedia which have the same meaning to query entity mention increases slowly. We choose 3 as the number of candidate articles based on the statistics in Fig. 3 and get a precision of 94.6 % based on our entity disambiguation module.

Evaluation of Cross-Lingual Entity Linking. Cross-lingual entity linking module is the core module in our framework. we compare our method with two state-of-the-art cross-lingual linking methods based on CLD. These methods are SVM-S based on the work of Sorg and Cimiano [12] and linkage factor graph model(LFG) based on the work of Wang et al. [15].

- **SVM-S.** This method treat cross-lingual entity linking as a classification problem, and train a SVM with some graph-based and text-based features between Wikipedia articles. They consider the top-k candidates with the respect to a ranking determined on the basis of the distance from the SVM-induced hyperplane.

Table 1. Experiment of cross-lingual entity linking (%).

Model	Precision	recall	F1
SVM-S	68.3	66.9	67.59
LFG	99.1	38.03	54.97
RSVM-G	68.18	69.84	69
RSVM-N	76.3	71.9	74.03
RSVM-Y	89.42	80.47	84.7

Table 2. Contribution analysis of different factors

(a) Semantic factors analysis(%)

Ignored Factor	Precision	recall	F1
Wiki full text	6.35	1.3	3.76
Wiki brief	**6.5**	**1.6**	**3.98**

(b) Graph-based factors analysis(%)

Ignored Factor	Precision	recall	F1
inlink	1.4	0.3	0.83
outlink	11.44	8.49	9.9
category	**20.9**	**15.1**	**17.9**

- **Linkage Factor Graph Model (LFG).** This method presents a factor graph model, and defines some structure features and constraint feature to describe the article in Wikipedia and the relations between articles in two language version of Wikipedia.

Because we have extracted 450 thousand English-Chinese wikipedia article pairs (KCL), so we set up RSVM-Y and RSVM-N. RSVM-Y adds links in KCL into our module, and RSVM-N not. As shown in Fig. 2, the structure information is less and less important for the new articles in Wikipedia. Model like LFG could not deal with these articles. So, we set up RSVM-G to evaluate our module.

Table 1 shows the performance of 3 different methods. According to the result, the LFG method gets really high precision of 99.1 %, but recall is only 38.03 %. Because LFG model ignores the entities with fewer structure features to other entities. RSVM-N outperforms SVM-S 6.44 % in terms of F1. By considering the known cross-lingual links, our method gets a precision of 89.42 %, and a recall of 80.47 %. Therefore, our RSVM model can discover more cross-lingual links, and performs better than SVM-S and LFG.

Overall Performance. We re-rank the 3 candidate YAGO entities by the score of Eq. (6), and get a 82.3 % query precision by CLEQS.

We perform an analysis to evaluate the contribution of different factors. We run RSVM-Y 5 times on evaluation data, and each time we remove one factor. Table 2(a) and Table 2(b) list the result of ignoring different factors. We find that the brief introduction of Wiki articles is more important than full text of Wiki articles. As shown in Table 2(b), outlink and category are more important than inlink in cross-lingual entity linking task. Because the category system changes less frequently than inlink and outlink, it is more important than inlink and outlink.

6   Conclusion

In this paper, we propose an approach for cross-lingual entity query from Chinese entity in text to the knowledge graph of YAGO. We have published a demo system [13] based on our approach. Our approach is made up of two modules: entity disambiguation module and cross-lingual entity linking module. Our approach uses the result of cross-lingual entity linking module to increase the precision of entity disambiguation module, and get a 82.3 % in query precision. We evaluate the core module and cross-lingual entity linking module, with other approaches. It shows that our approach can achieve higher precision and recall.

Acknowledgement. This work is supported by National Science Foundation of China under grant No. 61170086. The authors would also like to thank Ping An Technology (Shenzhen) Co., Ltd. for the support of this research.

References

1. Adafre, S.F., de Rijke, M.: Finding similar sentences across multiple languages in wikipedia. In: Proceedings of the 11th Conference of the European Chapter of the Association for Computational Linguistics, ECAL 2006, 3 April - 7 April 2006, Trento, Italy, pp. 62–69 (2006)
2. Albitar, S., Fournier, S., Espinasse, B.: An effective TF/IDF-based text-to-text semantic similarity measure for text classification. In: Benatallah, B., Bestavros, A., Manolopoulos, Y., Vakali, A., Zhang, Y. (eds.) WISE 2014, Part I. LNCS, vol. 8786, pp. 105–114. Springer, Heidelberg (2014)
3. Auer, S., Bizer, C., Kobilarov, G., Lehmann, J., Cyganiak, R., Ives, Z.G.: DBpedia: a nucleus for a Web of open data. In: Aberer, K., Choi, K.-S., Noy, N., Allemang, D., Lee, K.-I., Nixon, L.J.B., Golbeck, J., Mika, P., Maynard, D., Mizoguchi, R., Schreiber, G., Cudré-Mauroux, P. (eds.) ASWC 2007 and ISWC 2007. LNCS, vol. 4825, pp. 722–735. Springer, Heidelberg (2007)
4. Bagga, A., Baldwin, B.: Entity-based cross-document coreferencing using the vector space model. In: Proceedings of the Conference on 36th Annual Meeting of the Association for Computational Linguistics and 17th International Conference on Computational Linguistics, COLING-ACL 1998, 10–14 August, 1998, Université de Montréal, Montréal, pp. 79–85. Quebec, Canada (1998)
5. Bunescu, R.C., Pasca, M.: Using encyclopedic knowledge for named entity disambiguation. In: Proceedings on 11th Conference of the European Chapter of the Association for Computational Linguistics, EACL 2006, 3–7 April, 2006, Trento, Italy (2006)
6. Cristianini, N., Shawe-Taylor, J.: An Introduction to Support Vector Machines and Other Kernel-based Learning Methods. Cambridge University Press, New York (2010)

7. Jiang, L., Wang, J., An, N., Wang, S., Zhan, J., Li, L.: GRAPE: a graph-based framework for disambiguating people appearances in web search. In: ICDM 2009, The Ninth IEEE International Conference on Data Mining, Miami, Florida, USA, 6–9 December 2009, pp. 199–208 (2009)

8. Joachims, T.: Optimizing search engines using clickthrough data. In: Proceedings of the Eighth ACM SIGKDD International Conference on Knowledge Discovery and Data Mining, 23–26 July, 2002, Edmonton, Alberta, Canada, pp. 133–142 (2002)

9. Mahdisoltani, F., Biega, J., Suchanek, F.M.: YAGO3: a knowledge base from multilingual wikipedias. In: Seventh Biennial Conference on Innovative Data Systems Research, CIDR 2015, Asilomar, CA, USA, January 4–7, 2015, Online Proceedings (2015)

10. Miller, G.A.: Wordnet: a lexical database for english. Commun. ACM **38**(11), 39–41 (1995)

11. Shen, W., Wang, J., Luo, P., Wang, M.: LINDEN: linking named entities with knowledge base via semantic knowledge. In: Proceedings of the 21st World Wide Web Conference 2012, WWW 2012, Lyon, France, 16–20 April, 2012, pp. 449–458 (2012)

12. Sorg, P., Cimiano, P.: Enriching the crosslingual link structure of wikipedia - a classification-based approach. In: Proceedings of the Aaai Workshop on Wikipedia and Artifical Intelligence (2008)

13. Su, Y., Zhang, C., Cheng, W., Qian, W.: Cleqs: a cross-lingual entity query system based on knowledge graphs. In: NDBC 2015, Chengdu, China (2015)

14. Wang, C., Gao, M., He, X., Zhang, R.: Challenges in chinese knowledge graph construction. In: 31st IEEE International Conference on Data Engineering Workshops, ICDE Workshops 2015, Seoul, South Korea, 13–17 April, 2015, pp. 59–61 (2015)

15. Wang, Z., Li, J., Wang, Z., Tang, J.: Cross-lingual knowledge linking across wiki knowledge bases. In: Proceedings of the 21st World Wide Web Conference 2012, WWW 2012, Lyon, France, 16–20 April, 2012, pp. 459–468 (2012)

16. Wentland, W., Knopp, J., Silberer, C., Hartung, M.: Building a multilingual lexical resource for named entity disambiguation, translation and transliteration. In: Proceedings of the International Conference on Language Resources and Evaluation, LREC 2008, 26 May - 1 June 2008, Marrakech, Morocco (2008)

17. Witten, I.H., Milne, D.N.: An effective, low-cost measure of semantic relatedness obtained from wikipedia links. Proceedings of Aaai (2008)

18. Wu, W., Li, H., Wang, H., Zhu, K.Q.: Probase: a probabilistic taxonomy for text understanding. In: Proceedings of the ACM SIGMOD International Conference on Management of Data, SIGMOD 2012, Scottsdale, AZ, USA, 20–24 May, 2012, pp. 481–492 (2012)

Graph-Based Approach for Cross Domain Text Linking

Yu Hu, Tiezheng Nie[(⊠)], Derong Shen, and Yue Kou

College of Information Science and Engineering,
Northeastern University, Shenyang, China
huyuneu@163.com,
{nietiezheng, shenderong, kouyue}@mail.neu.edu.cn

Abstract. Comprehensive analysis of multi-domain texts has generated an important effect on text mining. Although the objects described by these multi-domain texts belong to different fields, they sometimes are overlapped partially; and linking these texts fragments which are overlapped or complementary is a necessary step for many tasks, such as entity resolution, information retrieval and text clustering. Previous works for computing text similarity mainly focus on string-based, corpus-based and knowledge-based approaches. However cross-domain texts exhibit very special features compared to texts in the same domain: (1) entity ambiguity, texts from different domains may contain various references to the same entity; (2) content skewness, cross domain texts are overlapped partially. In this paper, we propose a novel fine-grained approach based on text graph for evaluating the semantic similarity of cross-domain texts to link the similar parts. The experiment results show that our approach gives an effective solution to discover the semantic relationship between cross domain text fragments.

Keywords: Text graph · Cross domain text · Text linking · Semantic similarity

1 Introduction

Data integration technology is strongly influencing data analysis capacity in big data time for large amounts of multi-domains data with complementary expertise are semantic related. A comprehensive perspective on cross domain text can give researchers deep insight into text understanding. So linking the text fragments which describe the same object is important to many tasks. To identifying these semantic similarity texts from different domains, one should not only compute the relatedness between individual words but also consider the fundamental sentence structure.

Calculating the text similarity, a basic work in text mining and natural language processing, is an effective way to link these semantic similarity texts. Existing works always focus on full text semantic matching. But cross-domain texts are overlapped partially while we name this feature as content skewness. A global calculation method can't get an accurate result of similarity evaluation between cross-domain texts. At the same time, existing works use WordNet or Knowledge Base to quantify the degree to which word pairs are semantically related. But cross-domain texts contain various

© Springer International Publishing Switzerland 2015
R. Cai et al. (Eds.): APWeb 2015 Workshops, LNCS 9461, pp. 151–160, 2015.
DOI: 10.1007/978-3-319-28121-6_14

references to a same entity because researcher in different fields may have different convention in natural language.

In this paper, we propose a graph based approach to link the cross domain text fragments which describe the same object. Our approach leverages both the semantic similarity of words and the structural information of sentence. We propose a new method to compute semantic similarity between words to align word pairs. Then we take into full account the local similarity of texts and expand it to the global similarity. The structure we use is text graph containing individual words as its vertexes.

2 Related Work

As an important part of text mining, text semantic similarity has been studied for many years [1–3].

Previous works are mainly focus on string-based, semantic-based and corpus-based approaches. String-based approaches use the string similar degree algorithm directly, such as Jaccard Similarity [4], Levenshtein distance [5], etc. An interesting work measures the semantic similarity of texts combing the corpus-based word similarity and string similarity [1]. Their work focuses on the similarity between sentences. They propose a normalized and modified version of the Longest Common Subsequence (LCS) string matching algorithm.

Semantic-based algorithms mainly leverage external knowledge base, such as WordNet [6]. Jimenez et al. [7] introduce a novel strategy that considering the similarity of elements in a set. Samuel Fernando et al. [9] summarize six similarity metrics based on WordNet. Five of them use the information about the "is-a" hierarchy to compute the similarity. The remaining algorithm just uses the information about relatedness to compute the similarity.

Corpus-based algorithms try to evaluating the degree of similarity using the statistical information of large corpora. Mihalcea et al. [8] introduce two important corpus-based algorithms: point wise mutual information [10] and latent semantic analysis [11]. The pointwise mutual information is based on co-occurrence and statistical information computed from corpora set. The LSA is a classical approach for text analysis. Some word-frequency-based statistical approaches, such as PLSA [12] and LDA [13] can also reflect the complex latent semantic meaning in texts. PLSA add a priori information for LSA and LDA is a generative model for text modeling.

3 Semantic Similarity of Words

In this section, we introduce how we calculate the semantic similarity of words. Word embedding is a focused area of natural language processing research. Word embedding can cluster the semantically similar words. Here we show two word-to-word similarity metrics with word embedding results.

We conduct our evaluation using any chosen word embedding algorithm. With the help of neural network, word embedding algorithm can automatically learn better representation of words. It is a parameterized function mapping the words in literature to a high-dimensional vector space. In this vector space, semantic similar words are closer. Therefore we leverage the mapping space to define the semantic similarity of words.

Cosine similarity: Going to the source, we can find that the words embedding algorithm reflects the latent semantic similarity between words. Therefore, the value of cosine similarity obtained from the vector space can represent the similarity between two words.

Word similarity network: Inspired by the lexical-semantic network WordNet which is a semantic dictionary based on cognitive linguistics, we construct a word similarity network, in which a path represents the evolution process of related concept, to calculate the semantic similarity of words.

We suggest a simple but effective method for constructing the word similarity network. Suppose all the words have been mapped to a vector space with word embedding algorithm. First, selecting a word as the current point v, we pick out all the words semantic similar to this current word with a fixed threshold. We quantify the degree of semantic similarity with formula (1). Then we connect all the points representing the similar words with the current point. Then add these points to the vertex set V, add these connections to edge set E. At last, select a new point v' except for v in V as the new current point and repeat the above process until all the words are added in the network.

A path connecting two nodes describes the semantic evolution from one node to another. Here we propose a universal method to evaluate the similarity between any two words. The formula (2) is used to evaluate the similarity between words u and v. Here we utilize the shortest path between vector u and v because which indicates the fasted way their meaning changes. $D(u \rightarrow v) : v_1 v_2 \ldots v_i \ldots v_{k-1} v_k$: is the shortest path from u to v where v_1 is the vector u and v_k is the vector v.

$$w = \frac{\sum_{i=1}^{k} (a_i \times b_i)}{\sqrt{\sum_{i=1}^{k} a_i^2} \times \sqrt{\sum_{i=1}^{k} b_i^2}} \tag{1}$$

$$\text{sim}(u, v) = \prod_{i \in D(u \rightarrow v)} w(v_i, v_{i+1}) \tag{2}$$

Here, w means the similarity between two semantic similar words. a_i and b_i means the vector of the two words. v and u means any two words in the semantic similar network. It is possible that the final network is not connected. If there is no a path between two words, it means these two words are not semantic related so the similarity between any two words cannot be measured. We set this similarity score 0.

The basic hypothesis about this method is that the similarity score can be calculated by cosine similarity immediately if two words are similar or to say they may indicate the same entity. If two words are not similar, we can't simply apply the cosine similarity. So we use the evolution path between two words to describe their semantic similarity. Semantic association between words will decrease rapidly after a few steps in the graph. That is to say, in a limited distance two words may have high similarity. Some steps later, the similarity decrease rapidly.

4   Cross-Domain Text Linking

We propose a graph-based text fragments linking approach aiming at overcoming the entity ambiguity and content skewness of cross-domain texts. Our approach model texts as a graph and apply semantic similarity of words to local similarity of texts. Then we combine the local similarity into the structural information of texts to compute the global similarity of texts.

Our approach consists of three steps: word alignment using lexical semantic similarity; calculating the local similarity of text fragments; linking the texts that describe the same object.

4.1   Text Modeling

The efficiency and the ability of text feature expression make a text model good or not. The ability of text feature expression indicates whether the model can represent the text without the information loss. The efficiency indicates both the storage efficiency of text structure and time efficiency of text analysis. Here we use the graph model to represent the text. We build a graph to represent the text in which words with meaningful relations are connected with each other.

Vertices: text units of various sizes can be regarded as vertices in the text graph, such as words, phrases and expressions etc.

Edges: the relations between text units are added as edges in the text graph, such as co-occurrence, semantic similarity, etc. In this paper, we use the co-occurrence in a fixed window as the relation.

We construct the text graph as follows:

1. Identify the text units and add them in the vertices set. Individual word or phrases all can be used in our task.
2. Setting a fixed window with size n, if two text units have the co-occurrence relation in the window, draw a connection between them.

Node weight: text graph is built from natural language text, so we need a tool to evaluate how important a word is to a document in a corpus.

Edge weight: the edge weight represents the strength of connection between the vertices corresponding to the edge. While the relation between terms can be regarded as a symmetric relationship, we try to define a symmetric approach to represent the probabilistic correlation of words in text graph. We suppose that if two terms often appear in the same texts, they are more likely to have a high correlated relationship.

Tf-idf is the most popular method for weighting. Here we use an existing Eq. (3), a similar formula with tf-idf to weight the words.

$$w_{it} = \frac{ptf_{it}}{\sqrt{\sum_r ptf_{it}^2}} * \log \Phi_i \tag{3}$$

$$ptf_{it} = 0.5 + 0.5 * \frac{tf_{it}}{max_r tf_{rt}}, \quad \Phi_i = \frac{N}{n_i}, \tag{4}$$

Here w_{it} means the significance of the current word i in text t. tf_{it} is the occurrence frequency of term i in text t. Φ is the normal definition for Inverse Document Frequency. This formula means if a word appear in the a few texts but not appear in other texts it will be more important to these texts.

We introduce a new formula to evaluate the weight of an edge as (5).

$$\mathrm{cor}(s_i, s_j) = p_r(s_i|s_j) * p_r(s_i|s_j) \tag{5}$$

Here $p_r(s_i|s_j)$ means the probability that s_i appears in the texts where s_j belongs to. This formula represents the probabilistic that terms s_i and s_j appears in the same texts. $p_r(s_j|s_i)$ is as the same. In the text graph, the edge indicates that the vertices have the relation of co-occurrence. The weight of edge between nodes represents the correlation of text units.

4.2   Word Alignment and Feature Expansion

We calculate the semantic similarity of cross-domain texts T_1 and T_2 using word similarity to link them. For a word in T_1, we try to find the word in T_2 that has the highest similarity according to the algorithm we introduce in the previous section. Here we propose a greedy approach. For a word w_1 in T_1, find all the words in T_2 that has the highest similarity above the threshold. Figure 1 shows align words extracted for the text graph. Then these word pairs are regarded as align words to compute the semantic similarity of texts. We call the points that represent these words feature point.

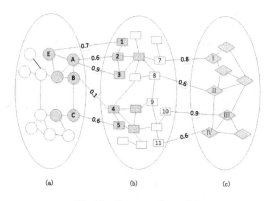

Fig. 1. Text graph model

For cross domain data always describe different objects, they use habitual natural language terms and edit the content they are interested in. So the texts are overlapped partially. Then we try to expand the common feature to the whole texts in the graph.

As what the shadow point shows in Fig. (1), we use a "from current point to adjacent point" strategy to expand the features. Our approach consist of two steps: (1) For each point that is a feature point in the text graph, we add its adjacent points to the feature point set; (2) add the edges that connect the feature points in the text graph to feature edge set. We suppose the words in the texts can be represented as text graph in Fig. (1), we pick out the aligned words pairs and add the aligned words and their adjacent points in the graph to the feature sets.

4.3   Cross-Domain Text Linking

Cross domain texts is different in their focus about the same object. We call the similarity between the partial coincident text fragments. So we consider this feature in full and propose an approach that utilizes the local similarity to calculate the global similarity of cross domain texts.

We utilize not only word-word similarity but also structure information of sentences. We convert simple word-word similarity to the combination model of words, which contains deeper levels of meaning like a lexicon or grammar information.

For two cross-domain text T_1 and T_2, their feature point set is P_1 and P_2. We define that the edge that connect two feature points is feature edge in the text graph. The feature edge set is E_1 and E_2. The local similarity between text fragments is computed as Eq. (6).

$$sim(EG_1, EG_2) = \frac{\sum_{(s_i,s_j) \in C} w_i * w_j * sim(s_i, s_j) * c\_cor}{\sqrt{\sum_{(s_i,s_j) \in EG_1} w_i^2 cor(s_i, s_j)} * \sqrt{\sum_{(s_i,s_j) \in EG_2} w_i^2 cor(s_i, s_j)}} \tag{6}$$

Here EG_1 and EG_2 are the extension sub graph. w_i and w_j are the node's weight of aligned words set C. For aligned words, we set the correlation to a constant $c\_cor = 1$.

This formula is based on the hypothesis that two similar fragments are more centralized in the cross domain texts. If the align words in the text pairs to be compared is not centralized, the cardinality of feature points remain the same, but the size of the feature edge set is become larger. So the local similarity degree of these texts becomes lower. This phenomenon is shown in Fig. 1 where feature points in (a) and (b) are centralized and feature points in (b) and (c) are not centralized. We can find that the extensional feature points generated by different points are overlapped. So they share a smaller set of feature points and feature edges.

Then we use sigmoid function to expand this local similarity to global similarity as formula (7) and (8).

$$k = \max\left(\frac{|EG_1|}{|T_1|}, \frac{|EG_2|}{|T_2|}\right) \tag{7}$$

$$f = \frac{1}{1 + e^{-\alpha(k-\beta)}} \tag{8}$$

In our experiment, we need a method to evaluate the contribution of the local similarity to global similarity. So we compute the coverage degree of the feature sub-graph to the original text graph. And if most of their words can be aligned or few of their words can be aligned, the computation of coverage degree will not affect the result. So we try to sharpen the computation where the coverage degree is between these two extremes to strengthen the ability to distinguish whether two texts are similar. Here α and β an be set to 5 and 0.5.

We link the texts if their similarity score as is shown in formula (9) is above a threshold.

$$\text{sim}(T_1, T_2) = f * \text{sim}(EG_1, EG_2) \tag{9}$$

Here $\text{sim}(T_1, T2)$ means the similarity degree between the two texts T_1 and $T2$. This formula shows how to convert the local similarity to global similarity.

5 Experiments

We conduct an experiment to the calculation of semantic similarity of words. We also conduct an experiment to link semantic similarity texts comparing with two classical algorithms. The real cross domain datasets we use in the experiment is academic thesis indexed by PubMed and United States patents. We use 189 patents and picked out 4146 articles from PubMed written by about 50 scientists in the field of medicine. We call the network constructed by Wikipedia as SimNet_wiki, and the network constructed by PubMed as SimNet_pub. Association Network (AN_free) [14] is very dependent on the anchor texts in Wikipedia. The statistic information contains five aspects: the size of the graph; average degrees for each node on the graph; the object of words that is described by the nodes.

We evaluate our approach on three aspects: Pearson product-moment correlation coefficient of semantic similarity word pairs; the result distribution of the text pairs in ground truth; the recall for cross-domain texts varying the threshold ρ and the size n of window in text graph.

First, we evaluate the correlation between the similar words we find by the three approaches. Table 1 shows the result on two test data.

Table 1. Pearson coefficient

	WordNet	AN_free	SN_wiki	SN_pub
WS-353	0.62	0.645	0.718	0.584
Biomed data	0.74	0.68	0.65	0.799

Then statistics result suggests that the distribution of the similarity score of text pairs in ground truth is concentrated above 0.6 as Fig. 2 shows. Cross-domain texts are not very semantic similar with each other so that measures of jaccard and semantic cosine similarity is not effective. But our approach, we name it as "textSim", takes full advantage of local similarity of the feature sub graph. We can see that this method observably have a high degree of differentiation between the linked texts and non-linked texts in ground truth. We quite don't find an effective state-of-the-art approach for cross-domain text fragments linking. So we choose jaccard, it is an easy but widely used approach for similarity calculating. And here the cosine similarity is an approach quite different from traditional cosine similarity. We take full consideration of the latent semantic similarity between words as its vectors. And we improve this equation to a symmetric version.

Then we evaluate how does size of window in text graph that affect the semantic similarity of cross-domain texts. Figure 3 show that when the size of the window in text graph is 3, the algorithm has the best performance. The reason for this is easy to understand. If the size of window is too small, the text graph tends to become a word bag or linear list. When the window's size is 1, the text graph model is equal to bag-of-words model. When the window's size is 2, the text graph model is equal to linear list model. If the size of window is too large, the text graph becomes a dense graph until a complete graph. When the text graph is too sparse or dense, the extended features are affected deeply. If the window's size is so large that the text graph becomes a complete graph, the feature points will be extended to all the text unit points so that this process loses all meaning.

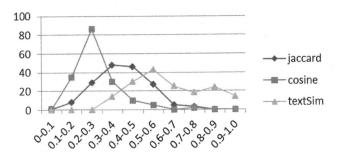

Fig. 2. Distribution of values of similarity calculation

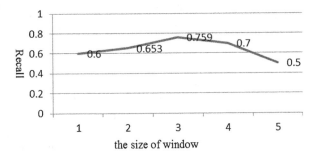

Fig. 3. Result influenced by the size of window

At last, we evaluate how the threshold ρ affect the similarity of short texts and long texts as is shown in Figs. 4 and 5. The threshold ρ is the sole criterion to determine whether two texts are similar and describe the same object. If the computation result is above ρ, we consider these two texts should be linked. And the way of feature extraction in our approach relies on the generated text graph. But short texts may not have an advantage in this model for short texts are not easy to build a representative text graph because they contains a small number of words and share little common words. So we try to exhibit the experiment result applying our algorithm on short/long texts independently.

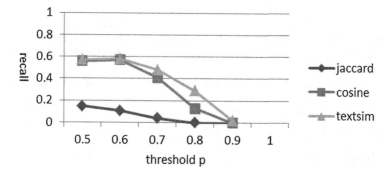

Fig. 4. Result for short texts

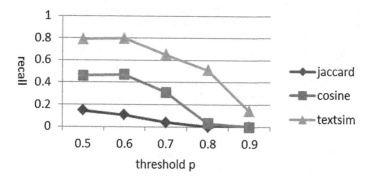

Fig. 5. Result for long texts

Here we use the titles of papers indexed by PubMed as the short text set, the abstract of papers as the long texts. The experiment result shows that the threshold ρ has a significant effect on cross domain texts linking. For short texts, text graph can't represent the connections; textSim performs the same with semantic Cosnine similarity algorithm. However out approach performs well signally for long texts. When the threshold $\rho = 0.6$, the approach has the best performance for both two data sets.

6 Conclusion

In this paper, we present a novel approach to evaluate the similarity between cross domain texts. Our approach models the relationship between words in document as a graph, which reflects both simantic relatedness of words and structure relatedness of sentences. The graph model works well on discovering the similarity between words or documents of cross domain.

References

1. Islam, A., Inkpen, D.: Semantic text similarity using corpus-based word similarity and string similarity. ACM Trans. Knowl. Disc. Data (TKDD) **2**(2), 10:1–10:25 (2008)
2. Gomaa, W.H., Fahmy, A.A.: A survey of text similarity approaches. Int. J. Comput. Appl. **68**(13), 13–18 (2013)
3. Zhan, Z., Yang, X., Computer, D.O., et al.: Text similarity calculation based on language network and semantic information. Comput. Eng. Appl. (2014)
4. Shameem, M.U.S., Ferdous, R.: An efficient k-means algorithm integrated with Jaccard distance measure for document clustering. In: First Asian Himalayas International Conference on Internet (AH-ICI 2009). IEEE, pp. 1–6 (2009)
5. Lan, Q.: Extraction of news content for text mining based on edit distance. J. Comput. Inf. Syst. **6**(11), 3761–3777 (2010)
6. Miller, G.A.: WordNet: a lexical database for English. Commun. ACM **38**(11), 39–41 (1995)
7. Jimenez, S., Gonzalez, F., Gelbukh, A.: Text comparison using soft cardinality. In: Chavez, E., Lonardi, S. (eds.) String Processing and Information Retrieval. Lecture Notes in Computer Science, vol. 6393, pp. 297–302. Springer, Heidelberg (2010)
8. Mihalcea, R., Corley, C., Strapparava, C.: Corpus-based and knowledge-based measures of text semantic similarity. In: National Conference on Artificial Intelligence, vol. 1, pp. 775–780 (2006)
9. Fern, S., Stevenson, M.A.: Semantic similarity approach to paraphrase detection. In: Computational Linguistics UK Annual Research Colloquium (2008)
10. Turney, P.: Mining the web for synonyms: PMI-IR versus LSA on TOEFL. In: Proceedings of the Twelfth European Conference on Machine Learning (ECML-2001) (2001)
11. Dumais, S.T.: Latent semantic analysis. Ann. Rev. Inf. Sci. Technol. **38**(1), 188–230 (2004)
12. Hofmann, T.: Probabilistic latent semantic analysis. In: Proceedings of the Fifteenth Conference On Uncertainty in Artificial Intelligence. Morgan Kaufmann Publishers Inc. (1999)
13. Blei, D.M., Ng, A.Y., Jordan, M.I.: Latent dirichlet allocation. J. Mach. Learn. Res. **3**, 993–1022 (2003)
14. Zhang, K., Zhu, K.Q., Hwang, S.-w.: An Association Network for Computing Semantic Relatedness (2015)

Multi-dimensional User Credibility Analysis on Review Content

Yifan Gao, Yuming Li, and Rong Zhang[✉]

Shanghai Key Laboratory of Trustworthy Computing,
Institute for Data Science and Engineering,
East China Normal University, Shanghai, China
{yfgao,ymli}@ecnu.cn, rzhang@sei.ecnu.edu.cn

Abstract. Traditionally, user credibility evaluation is calculated by comparing the overall measurements in rating systems. Actually, a user's rating against an item is different among aspects discussed in reviews. Then user credibility shall be discussed on aspect dimension instead of the overall evaluation dimension. To address this problem, we design a two-level model to analyze user credibility on aspects. Our method first detects all the involved aspects, and explores ratings for each aspect ratings by mining semantics in reviews. It makes full use of fine-grained information contains in comment text and can sensitively capture fluctuates among aspects. We model user scoring relationship by a weighted bipartite graph with users and aspects as nodes and credibility as weights. An iteration algorithm is designed for credibility calculation on the graph. We perform extensive experiments to demonstrate the advantages of our design.

1 Introduction

E-commerce sites provide ample platforms for customers to share their experiences on products or services. The space occupied by the reviews has been far beyond the description of products. These feedback information helps potential customers to judge products and make decisions. Good feedback from previous consumers will attract more orders. However, credibility of ratings from different users may be variant for many reasons, such as lack of experience in some domain and giving praise habitually/deliberately. These noise mixed in ratings and reviews will mislead purchasers to make inaccurate choice. Hence, it is crucial to learn the credibility of reviewers to evaluate products fairly.

Definition 1 (User Credibility on Aspects (UCA)). *It is defined as the evaluations to user i's ability giving reliable reviews d_i and ratings r_i on aspects a_k.*

Reviews are given with users' personal preference on various aspects. For example, when a person discusses a restaurant, he would express different profiles on taste, price, surroundings and service. Therefore, user credibilities on different

© Springer International Publishing Switzerland 2015
R. Cai et al. (Eds.): APWeb 2015 Workshops, LNCS 9461, pp. 161–170, 2015.
DOI: 10.1007/978-3-319-28121-6_15

aspects should be studied, rather than a total credibility value, to describe user profile. In this work, we explore UCA defined in Definition 1 by mining ratings and reviews. Realistic rating systems require users give an overall rating with a detailed description in review comments. Traditional methods, which only estimate a holistic ability of user giving reliable ratings, and consider nothing about the fine-grained information in comment text. In our approach, it can sensitively capture fluctuates among aspects which users concern about.

To address this problem, we propose an aspect-oriented credibility estimation algorithm to evaluate confidence believing user rating on an aspect. Firstly, it adopts a bootstrap method to detect aspects from review texts and learning the ratings on those aspects. Then, it designs an iterative algorithm based on a bipartite graph with users and aspects as nodes on each side and credibilities as weights between graph nodes. Compared with the work [10] most related to ours, we first present explicit aspects instead of latent topics discovered by probabilistic method [10] and it can present good explanation; second, we learn the rating for each aspect instead of using the overall rating for each latent topic [10], for different aspects have different ratings that can be mined from review content; third, there's a normalized equation to regulate and control aspect ratings according to the overall rating. Experiments on food dataset crawled from the biggest Chinese review site *Dianping*[1] demonstrate the advantage of our proposal over state-of-the-art solution.

2 Related Work

Spammer detection and expert finding are most typical researchs on user credibility. The former takes user linguistic features [10,13] and behavioral features [11,14,20] in to consideration to detect spammers who try to mislead readers with writing fake reviews. Many studies have been done on Web spam [3,16,19], Email spam [6], and social networks [7,9]. [8] is a supervised-based work typically on spam analysis and comes up with the assumption that duplicate reviews should be fake. [12] builds an unsupervised bayesian framework and formulates spammer detection as a clustering problem. [17] considers the relationship among reviews, reviewers and stores to present a graph-based method. On the contrary, expert finding aims at mining persons with rich experience who are supposed to produce truthful and reliable evaluations for a specific domain. Most of studies are based on the person local information [2,15] and relationships [22,24]. [1] shows a principal approach which is concentrated on capturing experts from all candidates. Language model applies in the process of identifying experts in [2]. [24] would like to find authoritative users with special knowledge for a relevant category in QA communities and they provided an extended category link graph and a topical link analysis approach.

However, spammer detection and expert finding are two kinds of extreme use cases for credibility detection. The most credible ones are expects and least credible ones are spammers. Between those two categories, it is said that there

---

[1] Dianping: http://www.dianping.com.

are users who may not be as strong as expects and as weak as spammers in their rating power. We can assign credibilities to those users and to adjust their ratings which affect product overall ratings finally. Most of the previous work [4, 5, 10, 23] emphasize on evaluate the quality of reviewers according to reviews and ratings. A simple but standard work, [23] designs a feedback mechanism to adjust customer credibility values. [4] combines reputation-based trust assessments and provenance information (i.e., how data has been produced) to determine trust values. The work most related to ours is [10]. It proposes a topic-biased model (TBM) to estimate user reputation and focuses on proving convergence. The first problem with TBM is that topics discovered by probabilistic method are abstract and difficult to generate user profile accurately. Secondly, they default topic distributions of review text as the degree which one item belongs to the topics. While topic distributions can't represent user credibilities on topics.

3   Methods

The major challenge in solving the problem is how to estimate UCA and coordinate the relationship between user ratings and item scores. We assume that reviewers give the overall rating based on a weighted combination of ratings on aspects which contain in review contents. We rate each aspect based on the semantic analysis to review content together with overall ratings. We design a two-fold model to realize the aim of UCA detection. As shown in Fig. 1, our model consists of two main components: *Semantic-based Rating Predictor* and *Aspect-oriented User Credibility Calculation*.

3.1   Semantic-Based Rating Predictor

The goal of this module is to map the sentences in a review into subsets corresponding to each aspect and predict aspect ratings according to the semantics of these sentences. There are three steps to obtain aspect ratings in each review:

- Split reviews into sentences and find the aspect inside. We have an assumption that each sentence covers only one aspect, such as taste, environment and service.
- Catch sentiment polarity for aspects. We need to find the sentimental words for each aspects.
- Rate each aspect. According to the sentimental words surrounding the aspect and the overall rating for the piece of review, we predict the rating for each aspect.

Aspect Extraction. Suppose each aspect can be described by a set of keywords and inside each sentence there is at most one aspect, we first extract describing keyword set for aspects. We design a boot-strapping algorithm to generate keywords for each aspect as shown in Algorithm 1. At the beginning, we give a set of seed words for each aspect. The boot-strapping algorithm appends words with

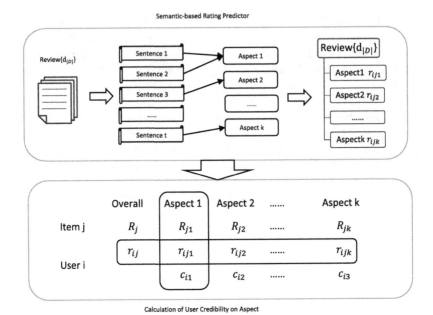

Fig. 1. Flowchart

high dependencies to the corresponding aspect keyword list and repeats dependency calculation until the aspect keyword list is unchanged by iteration from 2 to 5. We match the aspect keywords in each sentence, the sentence is assigned to an aspect with the maximum matching hits as 3. The result of boot-strapping algorithm is a t sentences corresponding table with k aspects labels.

Aspect Polarity. Different from [18], we support that word sentiment polarities is the most important factor that determines aspect ratings rather than the model parameters. Using the existed aspect ratings, we can obtain own sentiment polarity dictionary based on the statistical relationship between words in aspect and ratings. This dictionary is general. Lacking of aspect ratings data set, it can reference Chinese sentiment polarity dictionary, e.g. NTUSD made by National Taiwan University. The polarity p of one word w_n on the aspect A_k depends on the aspect rating r_k of the sentences x_t which contains this word. We measure the word sentiment polarity as:

$$p_{nk} = \frac{1}{T} \sum_{t=1}^{T} r_{kt}, p_{nk} \in [1,5] \tag{1}$$

(3) Predicting aspect ratings of each review

Semantic-based rating predictor aims at discovering the aspect ratings in each individual review based on semantics in review contents. In our model, the

---

Algorithm 1. Boot-strapping Algorithm

Input:

A collection of reviews $\{d_1, d_2, ..., d_{|D|}\}$,

sets of aspect seedwords $\{A_1, A_2, ..., A_k\}$,

selection threshold p, iterative step limited s and weight times t;

Output:

t sentences in a review corresponded with k aspects labels.

1: Split all reviews into sentences $X = \{x_1, x_2, ..., x_t\}$, split each sentence into words $W = \{w_1, w_2, ..., w_n\}$, and set the correlation $\mathcal{C}$ of seedwords as ∞ and other words as 0;

2: Match aspect keywords in each sentence of X;

3: Assign the sentence an aspect label by $\sum_W \mathcal{C}(w_n)$. If there is a tie, the sentence neither belongs to any aspect and waits for next iteration;

4: Calculate $\mathcal{X}^2$ according to [21] as the correlation of each words to aspects;

5: Rank the words under each aspect with respect to their $\mathcal{X}^2$ value and join the top p words for each aspect into their corresponding aspect keyword list A_k, and remove the word from current aspect, if t times correlated to another;

6: Iterate from 3 to 5 until the aspect keyword list is unchanged or iteration exceeds s;

---

review text is divided into sentences and each sentence is treated as a semantic unit. So, we first calculate the rating of sentences r_t which belong to the aspect k. The aspect rating r_k takes the average of sentences ratings r_{kn} as follows:

$$r_{kt} = \frac{1}{N} \sum_{n=1}^{N} p_{nk} \tag{2}$$

$$r_k = \frac{1}{T} \sum_{t=1}^{T} r_{kt} \tag{3}$$

3.2 Calculation of User Credibility on Aspect

Generally, the rating of an item is averaged with all users having equal weights. Adding the credibility factor can improve accuracy by reducing the influence of unreliable user. Designing a credibility-based algorithm, we estimate item scores and user aspect credibilities iteratively. If user u always give ratings closed to item true rating, u will have high credibility, and vice versa. In our model, the item score is derived from a total of weighted average of users' ratings.

Given a set of user U and a set of item V, R_{jk} is the kth aspect rating of the item j and $\{r_{ij}(i \in Uj \in V)\}$ represents the overall rating user i gives to item j. c_{ik} is defined as the kth aspect credibility of user i. The iterative calculation method is defined as follows:

$$R_{jk}^{s+1} = \frac{1}{|M_j|} \sum_{u_i \in M_j} r_{ijk} c_{ik}^{'s} \tag{4}$$

$$c_{ik}^{s+1} = 1 - D(\{r_{ijk}, R_{jk}^{s+1}\}_{V_j \in N_i}) \tag{5}$$

$$c_{ik}^{'s+1} = \frac{c_{ik}^{s+1}}{\frac{\sum_k c_{ik} r_{ijk}}{K \cdot r_{ij}}} \tag{6}$$

where M_j is the set of users who have rated v_j , N_i is the set of items that u_i has rated and s is the round of iteration. $D(\{r_{ijk}, R_{jk}^{s+1}\}_{V_j \in N_i})$ is a divergence measurement function to calculate the distance between user rating and item score.Obviously, the value of credibility the more close to 1, user credibility is better.

Compared with the traditional method, the product of the user's rating and the credibility coefficient is considers as the user real rating. At the end of each iteration, we design a correction in consideration of that the overall rating has a hold on aspect ratings. As shown in Fig. 1, not only the vertical relationship between the rating and credibility is considered, we also consider the feedback of the overall rating on horizontal.

4   Experiments

In this section, we first introduce the review data set used for experiments and then discuss the result of aspect rating prediction and UCA evaluation separately.

4.1   Data Set

We crawl the review data from Dianping which is the biggest restaurant review site to evaluate the performance of our system. There are totally 94,143 restaurants in Shanghai area and only 21,553 restaurants having reviews. Filtering out shops with reviews less than 20, our dataset consists of 576,990 reviews came from 8,988 restaurants. In order to ensure that reviews can completely express aspects, we require each reviews containing at least 4 sentences and each sentence having at least 5 words. Meet the above conditions, there are 7,611 restaurants. Sentence segmentation can obtain 5,128,114 sub-sentences containing 194,219 distinct words. Besides the overall rating, reviewers also provided 3 aspect ratings: taste, surroundings and service which take value from $\{1, 2, ..., 5\}$. On the one hand, these ratings can serve as ground-truth for quantitative evaluation of aspect rating prediction. On the other hand, this part of dataset are not required imperatively which leads data sparsity and let it necessary to predict aspect ratings.

4.2   Semantic-Based Aspect Rating Prediction

The baseline of this session is [18] which is a probabilistic rating regression model to analyze individual reviewer's latent opinion on aspects in reviews. Different from ours, they apply a Latent Rating Regression (LRR) model to learn aspect ratings and aspect weights. The implementation of LARA is available online[2]. Because of Chinese dataset, LARA has necessary modules to convert Chinese text documents to bag-of-words representation. We user Ansj[3] which is an open source for Chinese segmentation and part-of-speech tagging instead of OpenNLP.

We report the Aspect Mean Square Error (AMSE) of the rating predictor and it is defined as:

$$AMSE = \frac{1}{K \times |D|} \sum_{d=1}^{|D|} \sum_{a=1}^{K} (\hat{r}_{da} - r_{da})^2, \tag{7}$$

$$MAE = \frac{1}{K \times |D|} \sum_{d=1}^{|D|} \sum_{a=1}^{K} |\hat{r}_{da} - r_{da}|, \tag{8}$$

where K is the size of aspects, $|D|$ is the amount of reviews, $\hat{r}_{da}$ and r_{da} are the predicted rating and the user assigned rating scores in review d on aspect a, respectively. The comparison is listed in Table 1. Reading the result, LARA seems to be unsuited for processing our dataset. Our method has better performance and it proves our method wins a comparatively accurate prediction based on semantic analysis to review content.

Table 1. Results of rating prediction on dianping data

	AMSE	MAE
Ours	1.24	0.92
LARA	1.56	1.53

4.3   Calculation of User Credibility on Aspect

$D(\cdot)$ needs to meet the demand of evaluation rating distance. We do not use L1 distance as used in [10], and express formula (5) as (9) which can avoid the selection of parameters.

$$c_{ik}^{s+1} = (1 - \frac{r_{ijk} - R_{jk}}{r_{ijk}}) \times \frac{R_j}{r_{ij}} \tag{9}$$

As mentioned in the related work, TBM [10] proposed six topic-biased model to estimate User Reputation (UR) in terms of different topics as well as item

---

[2] http://sifaka.cs.uiuc.edu/~wang296/Codes/LARA.zip.
[3] http://www.ansj.org/.

scores and it is the work having common goals. We compare the best one (TB-L1-AVG) of the six models described in their paper with ours. The damping factor λ is fit to set as 0.2. The evaluation functions: Root Mean Square Error (RMSE) and Mean Absolutely Error (MAE) are defined as:

$$RMSE = \frac{1}{K \times |D|} \sqrt{\sum_{k=1}^{K} \sum_{d=1}^{|D|} (r_{ijk} c_{ik} - R_{jk})^2_{i,j \in |D|}}, \tag{10}$$

$$MAE = \frac{1}{K \times |D|} \sum_{k=1}^{K} \sum_{d=1}^{|D|} |r_{ijk} c_{ik} - R_{jk}|_{i,j \in |D|}, \tag{11}$$

where r_{ijk} and R_{jk} are ratings user i gives to shop j on aspect k and shop j scored on aspect k while c_{ik} is user i credibility on aspect k. The results are shown in Table 2. Obviously, the result of user ratings combined with credibility is really closed to shop scores.

Table 2. Results of learning user credibility on aspects

	MAE	RMSE
Ours	0.69	0.83
TB-L1-AVG	0.82	1.34

5   Conclusion

User credibility plays an essential role in estimating item scores. We propose a two-level model to analyze user credibility on aspects by mining the fine-grained information in the review text. Designing a boot-strapping algorithm combining with sentiment polarity dictionary splits review into aspect dimensions. Aspect credibilities are regarded as the weights of user ratings to calculate item score iteratively. Experiments show that the measure of credibility is accurate comparatively.

Acknowledgment. This work is partially supported by National Science Foundation of China (Grant No. 61232002, 61402180), and Program for Innovative Research Team in Yunnan University under grant No. XT412011.

References

1. Balog, K., Azzopardi, L., De Rijke, M.: Formal models for expert finding in enterprise corpora. In: Proceedings of the 29th Annual International ACM SIGIR Conference on Research and Development in Information Retrieval, pp. 43–50. ACM (2006)

2. Balog, K., Azzopardi, L., de Rijke, M.: A language modeling framework for expert finding. Inf. Process. Manage. **45**(1), 1–19 (2009)
3. Castillo, C., Donato, D., Becchetti, L., Boldi, P., Leonardi, S., Santini, M., Vigna, S.: A reference collection for web spam. In: ACM Sigir Forum. vol. 40, pp. 11–24. ACM (2006)
4. Ceolin, D., Groth, P.T., Van Hage, W.R., Nottamkandath, A., Fokkink, W.: Trust evaluation through user reputation and provenance analysis. In: URSW, vol. 900, pp. 15–26 (2012)
5. Chen, B.C., Guo, J., Tseng, B., Yang, J.: User reputation in a comment rating environment. In: Proceedings of the 17th ACM SIGKDD International Conference on Knowledge Discovery and Data Mining, pp. 159–167. ACM (2011)
6. Chirita, P.A., Diederich, J., Nejdl, W.: Mailrank: using ranking for spam detection. In: Proceedings of the 14th ACM International Conference on Information and Knowledge Management, pp. 373–380. ACM (2005)
7. Ghosh, S., Viswanath, B., Kooti, F., Sharma, N.K., Korlam, G., Benevenuto, F., Ganguly, N., Gummadi, K.P.: Understanding and combating link farming in the twitter social network. In: Proceedings of the 21st International Conference on World Wide Web, pp. 61–70. ACM (2012)
8. Jindal, N., Liu, B.: Opinion spam and analysis. In: Proceedings of the 2008 International Conference on Web Search and Data Mining, pp. 219–230. ACM (2008)
9. Kolari, P., Java, A., Finin, T., Oates, T., Joshi, A.: Detecting spam blogs: A machine learning approach. In: Proceedings of the National Conference on Artificial Intelligence. vol. 21, p. 1351. AAAI Press, MIT Press, London, Cambridge (2006)
10. Li, B., Li, R.H., King, I., Lyu, M.R., Yu, J.X.: A topic-biased user reputation model in rating systems. Knowl. Inf. Syst. **44**, 581–607 (2014)
11. Li, F., Hsieh, M.H.: An empirical study of clustering behavior of spammers and group-based anti-spam strategies. In: CEAS (2006)
12. Mukherjee, A., Kumar, A., Liu, B., Wang, J., Hsu, M., Castellanos, M., Ghosh, R.: Spotting opinion spammers using behavioral footprints. In: Proceedings of the 19th ACM SIGKDD International Conference on Knowledge Discovery and Data Mining, pp. 632–640. ACM (2013)
13. Ntoulas, A., Najork, M., Manasse, M., Fetterly, D.: Detecting spam web pages through content analysis. In: Proceedings of the 15th International Conference on World Wide Web, pp. 83–92. ACM (2006)
14. Ramachandran, A., Feamster, N.: Understanding the network-level behavior of spammers. ACM SIGCOMM Comput. Commun. Rev. **36**(4), 291–302 (2006)
15. Serdyukov, P., Hiemstra, D.: Modeling documents as mixtures of persons for expert finding. In: Macdonald, C., Ounis, I., Plachouras, V., Ruthven, I., White, R.W. (eds.) ECIR 2008. LNCS, vol. 4956, pp. 309–320. Springer, Heidelberg (2008)
16. Spirin, N., Han, J.: Survey on web spam detection: principles and algorithms. ACM SIGKDD Explor. Newsl. **13**(2), 50–64 (2012)
17. Wang, G., Xie, S., Liu, B., Yu, P.S.: Review graph based online store review spammer detection. In: IEEE 11th International Conference on Data Mining (ICDM), pp. 1242–1247. IEEE (2011)
18. Wang, H., Lu, Y., Zhai, C.: Latent aspect rating analysis on review text data: a rating regression approach. In: Proceedings of the 16th ACM SIGKDD International Conference on Knowledge Discovery and Data Mining, pp. 783–792. ACM (2010)
19. Wu, B., Goel, V., Davison, B.D.: Topical trustrank: using topicality to combat web spam. In: Proceedings of the 15th International Conference on World Wide Web, pp. 63–72. ACM (2006)

20. Wu, C.H.: Behavior-based spam detection using a hybrid method of rule-based techniques and neural networks. Expert Sys. Appl. **36**(3), 4321–4330 (2009)
21. Yang, Y., Pedersen, J.O.: A comparative study on feature selection in text categorization. In: ICML, vol. 97, pp. 412–420 (1997)
22. Zhang, J., Ackerman, M.S., Adamic, L.: Expertise networks in online communities: structure and algorithms. In: Proceedings of the 16th International Conference on World Wide Web, pp. 221–230. ACM (2007)
23. Zhang, R., Gao, M., He, X., Zhou, A.: Learning user credibility for product ranking. Knowl. Inf. Sys. (2014)
24. Zhu, H., Chen, E., Xiong, H., Cao, H., Tian, J.: Ranking user authority with relevant knowledge categories for expert finding. World Wide Web **17**(5), 1081–1107 (2014)

Author Index

Printed in the United States
By Bookmasters